THE
WINTERTON
STORY

THE
WINTERTON
STORY

by
David Higgins

PHOENIX PUBLICATIONS

Published in 2009 by Phoenix Publications
Walnut Farm, Beech Crescent, West Winch,
King's Lynn, Norfolk, PE33 0PZ.
Tel: 01553 840447

Origination and printing by
DSD Printers, King's Lynn, Norfolk Tel: 01553 661166.

British Library Cataloguing in Publication Data
A catalogue record for this book is available from the British Library

ISBN 978-0-9540684-3-1

Contents

Acknowledgements

I would like to express my gratitude to the following people and organisations that, in one way or another, have assisted in the production of this book, including the provision of illustrations.

The Great Yarmouth Library, the Norwich Library, the Norfolk Record Office and the National Archives.

Past research:

Jimmy Brown, Stanley Chaston, Josephine Dix, Sidney Empson, Ada Fakes, Ruth Gallant, Alec George, Ann George, Betty George, Edna George, John George, Kitty George, William Goffin, Roger Goffin, Tommy Goffin, Bob Green, Edith Green, Ella Green, Eddie Green, John Green, Olive Grimes, Ina Hagan, Michael Harvey, Bob Haylett, Stanley Hewitt, Margaret Hidden, Bob King, Dick King, John King, Ruby King, Ray Larner, Val Larner, Winnie Larner, Donald Leech, George Leech, Marjorie Leech, Selina Leech, Benedicta Osborne, Eddie Powles, Walter Rudd, Jim Todd, Geoffrey Wacey, Parry Watson, George Woodhouse, and Myrtle Woodhouse.

Recent research:

Kate Findlay, Christine Gee, Sandra Laws, Bob Malster, and Brian Rudd.

Jane Whiskens at DSD Printers.

Sheila West for typing the manuscript and general assistance as part of the Phoenix Publications team.

Brenda, my wife, for proof reading.

This Book is dedicated to all those Winterton men and women who over the years toiled endlessly to wrest a living from the sea.

PREFACE

Winterton holds a special place in the maritime history of East Anglia. Situated close to the North Sea it stood sentinel over the northern approach to the Yarmouth Roads and the promontory known as Winterton Ness, a hazard dreaded by all sailors plying their trade along the East Coast. It was also a short distance from the country's premier herring fishing port, Great Yarmouth. These factors combined to nurture a community of hardy nautical jacks-of-all-trades who for centuries strived to make a living from fishing and salvaging.

Being born and brought up in Great Yarmouth I was aware of that town's maritime heritage and later discovered ancestors who had worked in a number of seafaring activities, but of Winterton I knew very little until the early 1970s, when I started researching my wife's family history. With her forebears having lived there for generations it soon became clear that their story was inseparable from that of the village. This prompted me to widen the scope of the documentary research and carry out a series of interviews with those in the village who still remembered the 'old days and the old ways'.

It was always my intention to use this material to write a book about the village, but during an interview with John Starchy George Jnr., I was introduced to the Beach Companies, a term completely new to me. As he reminisced so my imagination was fired, but when I tried to find out more about these interesting organisations I discovered that very little had been written about them. As a result the Winterton project was shelved while I researched and wrote The Beachmen, which was published in 1987.

With other demands keeping me occupied I did not return to the story of Winterton until August 2008 when I was approached by Sandra Laws to give a talk on the village, to boost the church restoration fund. Viewing this as a timely prompt, I decided to complete the task I had set myself over 30 years ago.

The book is divided into six time periods within which a number of themes are developed, namely; 'longshore fishing, deep-sea fishing, salvaging, lifesaving, village life, and village development. Naturally enough the emphasis is strongly nautical, but I have not forgotten that, with the parish land being so fertile, there was always a significant farming presence, with some families being more associated with working the land than the sea. Farming, however, is a relatively passive activity, with none of the drama that goes with seafaring. It has not, therefore, been treated as a main theme.

Whilst this book has been written to appeal to anyone with an interest in Winterton, I have tried to include, for the benefit of family historians, as many photographs as possible of named individuals and, for the boat enthusiast, a comprehensive record of Winterton owned sailing boats and steam drifters.

On the subject of photographs I am always looking to expand my Winterton collection, especially with photos from the 19th Century. If anyone has any they think might interest me I would be very pleased to hear from them.

David Higgins
February 2009

1

1. Robert 'Tuscan' Hodds, inspecting a hand held shrimp net, c1900.

2. Charles Larner, father of Wilks, the 'Fisher King of Yarmouth', c1905.

3. Simon Gunton Kettle, on the sea-bank, c1900.

4. Elizabeth Hodds nee Smith, braiding a net, c1890.

1. ORIGIN AND EARLY DAYS

Winterton lies a few feet above sea level, on the north-eastern corner of the 'Island' of Flegg. On its seaward side it is protected by a substantial marram covered sea-bank and to the north there is an area of reclaimed marsh, formerly a warren and now a nature reserve. To the south-east the village nestles against the northern tip of the Flegg coastal cliff and to the west are East Somerton and West Somerton.

It has long been recognised that Winterton and Somerton were once closely related, both probably starting life as seasonal encampments established by people from a nearby village, sometime before the Danes made the Flegg a Danish island.[1] Martham is the most likely candidate for the parent village, with Somerton being the camp used in summer by those grazing livestock on the nearby marshes and Winterton that resorted to in winter by those seeking to exploit the white fish stocks and the autumn herring shoals. Over the years these seasonal camps hardened into permanent settlements and later became the basis for three separate parishes.

Winterton is first mentioned by name in an Anglo-Saxon charter of 1044-7,[2] but it is the Domesday survey of 1086 which gives the earliest insight into the village as a community.[3] In all 58 men were recorded, representing the heads of households of a population of around 250 people. These men farmed 334 acres with nine ploughs and also had access to 11 acres of meadow. As far as livestock is concerned only six pigs were mentioned and there was a salt works shared with another unspecified village.

This description is that of a simple farming community, there being no mention of seafaring. This is probably because the survey was concerned with fixed manorial economic activity, whereas fishing was more transient and open to everyone. As such it was not a direct source of manorial income, other than at Yarmouth where 24 fishermen were recorded. It can safely be assumed that fishing did take place from Winterton at this time and had done so for centuries.

The five manorial lords who gained benefit from the land and the people of Winterton in 1086 were William I, Roger Bigot, the Bishop of Thetford, the Abbot of Holme, and William de Ecouis. The estates they held were valuable assets, the farmland being described in 1600 in the following terms; 'The grounds about it (Winterton) are in the opinion of many most fruitfull fatte & mouldie of any pt in England for unto the tillage it requireth the least labour as one horse though but a jade & yet yeildeth the greatest plenty of Corne'.[4]

Over the centuries these manorial holdings changed hands or were sub-let, passing down through such families at the de Mautebys, de Fleggs, de Begviles and de Cleres to Sir John Fastolf, the Pastons, and the Woodhouses of Waxham. By the end of the 18th Century the principal landowners were the Earl of Winterton (Edward Turnour), Lord Braybrooke (Richard Neville), and John Barker Huntington. As none of these men were resident it fell to one of their tenants, or the rector, to assume the role of 'father of the village' at any given time.

Whilst the Domesday Survey is silent on seafaring activity there are sufficient references in other early sources to make good the deficit. Barbara Cornford, in her book Medieval Flegg, states that; 'By the fourteenth Century fishing from Winterton was important enough for the Crown to have established a toll on boats. In 1334-5 the Hemsby Manorial Accounts record the receipt of 5s 6d from the tolls of eleven boats at Winterton, and later in the fourteenth Century Dionysia Clere of Ormesby claimed 'Havencourtes', which is described as a Botetoll in Winterton'.[5]

She also records that Clement Paston went to Winterton from Paston to sell his grain and that in the early 15th Century John Locke, a Winterton crayerman, was buying malt from the Ormesby manor, for export or coastal trade.

Less surprising is the fact that there were fish merchants operating in the village. In 1360

5. Beach Road, looking west, towards the church, c1875.

Edward III sent an order to the bailiffs responsible for the Yarmouth herring fair to regulate the purchase of herring by the merchants from the 'fishers'. In this mention is made of the merchants of Winterton buying fish to serve 'the carts and horses that shall come there from divers counties'.[6]

In 1401, John Wyneton, a London fish merchant (originally from Winterton?) appealed a decision made against him at the Court of Admiralty. The case was one of breach of contract brought by three Winterton men, Richard Brown, John Topy and John Stuteville, in relation to freighting a ship called *La Piers* of Winterton. Wyneton had been ordered to pay £300 damages and costs.

In 1565, with Britain at war with Spain, a survey of boats and sailors was taken.[7] For Winterton the entry reads; 'Ther are belonginge to the said towne boates occupied in heringe faire onely to ye Number of 6'. These were the *Edmund* and the *John* owned by Edmund Cobbe, the *Margaret*, owned by Thomas Lyghton, the *Fortune*, owned by William Johnson, the *John*, owned by William Swanton and yet another *John*, owned by John Woodes. These boats were relatively small, five being of four tonns burthen, the other five. Crewing them were six mariners and eight fishermen. For the village as a whole there were 24 households occupying as many houses. The findings of this survey suggest that in the early part of Elizabeth I's reign Winterton was much smaller than it had been hitherto.

Towards the end of the same reign mariner John Barleye died and the probate inventory of his goods gives the first detailed account of what a Winterton fisherman/fish merchant needed to operate his business.[8] He was clearly a man of local significance, occupying a substantial house and a range of outbuildings, including a brewery.

In his storehouse were 20 martlemass nets (for herring fishing), 45 pieces of mackerel net, a dazing net and various ropes and corks. His great fish house contained eight cade of red herring and in another building were four lines, two dannes and a bowl anchor. There were also 12 old

4

swills in the wine house. In the yard was a hurry-curry (cart), a boat called the *Grace* with her tackle, and a small two-oared boat. Upstairs in the house he kept a sword, 'two bowes of ewe and on(e) handgune called a currier' and some arrows. One wonders if three years earlier, when the Spanish Armada had set sail, he had been ready to put them to good use.

In 1664, on the eve of the first Anglo-Dutch war, another survey of seamen was taken.[9] For Winterton 29 men were named, 9 of whom were described as 'Impressmen nowe in service'. Those forced to serve were young, unmarried men among whom was Clement Trotter. His father, of the same name, was the light keeper in the village. Trotter senior died in 1686 and his will describes him as a mariner. He left several houses and his gravestone stands against the church porch. It has the distinction of being the oldest in the churchyard.

Christopher Leaker (Leake, Lake), another impressed man, died in 1712. He was also a mariner and he was of sufficient standing to leave land and houses. Of more interest to this brief survey of the early days is the fact that an inventory of his goods detailed his fishing gear.[10] He owned a sea boat, with an anchor, cable and oars valued at £2 15s.0d a sett net, anchor, two stalls, buoys and buoy ropes and two barrels worth £3; five herring nets, a tow and bowl worth £1; 21 fishing lines, two small tows and two danns worth £1 10s.0d; and two didles, a boat hook and two small anchors worth 5s.0d. He also owned a cow and a pig.

As far as salvage was concerned, most manorial lords with land on the coast claimed 'wreck of sea', i.e. the right to anything washed up on the beach. Thomas de Begvile claimed this for his Winterton manor in 1331 and Robert de Clere did likewise in 1446, but it was not always easy to enforce these rights. In 1477 a 'grete chyppe' was wrecked off Winterton and the wreckage and cargo of timber was washed up on the shore. Winterton men John Longyard, Thomas Goodknape, Will Wrantham, and John Curteys, together with Robert Parker of West Somerton, carried much of it away, thereby infringing the wreck rights of Sir John Paston.[11]

6. Beach Road, looking east, c1875.

Off-shore salvage was also carried out in these early days. In 1344 there was a complaint made by Norwich merchants against 12 named men and others who had boarded a ship called the *busse de Norwege* off Winterton and carried away goods to the value of £500, as well as £100 in cash. Given that the case was not one of piracy it looks very much like an early example of beach company activity.

Likewise in 1452 the bailiffs of Yarmouth were directed to investigate the case of a hulk called *le Marie-Kneght* of Gdansk (then in Prussia), which had been wrecked near Winterton, as some of her merchandise had been salvaged. As her master, Matthew Schenekyn, his crew and some merchants had landed, it was claimed that the ship was not a wreck of sea and had therefore been plundered.

This brings us to the main cause of savage work, Winterton Ness. It is scarcely discernible today, but in the past the Ness was a very prominent feature. When in 1722 Daniel Defoe visited the coast near Winterton he described it as 'particularly famous for being one of the most dangerous and most fatal to the sailors in all England, I may say in all Britain; and the more so, because of the great number of ships which are continually going and coming this way, in their passage between London and all the northern coasts of Great-Britain'.[12]

The problem was that ships sailing the east coast would set a course between Winterton Ness and Flamborough Head (or vice versa) to keep them clear of the embayment centred on the Wash, but if the wind was blowing in any direction from the south-east to the north-west, masters would find it difficult to weather the Ness and their vessels could be driven ashore or onto a sandbank. This led to the introduction of measures to assist seamen and Defoe went on to say that; 'The dangers of this place being thus considered, 'tis no wonder, that upon the shore beyond Yarmouth, there are no less than four light houses kept flaming every night beside the lights at Caster,...'.[13]

7. Vessel ashore on the beach alongside 'a dangerous spot in the sea-banks', c1900.

8. 'View of the village and Lighthouse of Winterton'. Lithograph by J.B. Ladbrooke, c1825. Note the lighthouse, built in 1687, The Three Mariners Inn and Virginity Cottage above it on the cliff.

The lights he saw had had a chequered history, but not because the Winterton men did them any harm. There is no evidence that they behaved like the infamous Cornish wreckers. Being seamen they had an empathy with those afloat and in any case the volume of salvage work was such that there was no need. It is said, however, that the nightly prayer of a Winterton child was, 'Please God send father a good wreck before dawn.'

The growth in the coal-trade brought repeated calls for lights at Winterton. In 1600 the Trinity Brethren surveyed the Yarmouth Roads, but chose to site lights at Caister rather than Winterton. This did not satisfy the merchants, and in 1615 Sir William Erskine and Dr Welwood secured the agreement of James I to erect a light at the village, their motivation being to collect tolls from passing shipping.

The Trinity Brethren, however, had the sole right to place lights, so they swiftly mounted a legal challenge and took direct action by erecting what was called the Tower Lighthouse at Winterton. Overcoming the challenge, Erskine and his new partner, Sir John Meldrum, received a Royal patent and established two candle lights on the Ness and a fire light in the village.

Undaunted, the Trinity Brethren maintained their opposition and in 1621 a special court was convened to resolve the dispute. In the event the grant to Sir John, by then the sole proprietor, was confirmed and the Trinity Brethren were precluded from erecting any lights within two miles of Winterton. For the next 16 years Meldrum maintained a light in the village and two on the Ness, all working as a single navigational beacon. He then sold his interest to Alderman Gore of London.

This was the situation until the 1670s when violent storms shifted the sandbanks and created a new channel into the Yarmouth Roads. In 1677 a petition was presented to the Trinity Brethren calling for an additional lighthouse to be erected on the foreshore to serve as a front light to the existing Tower Light. They in turn were granted a patent to erect a new light.

9. 'Winterton Thwart Lights'. Engraving by William Henry Timms, c1820. The two light towers were demolished around 1830.

Unfortunately this was a period of coastal erosion, when the sea was constantly undermining the site of the new light. Eventually it was realised that it would have to be moved further back, but for this to happen the Tower Light, now in the hands of Sir Edward Turnour, would also have to be moved.

In 1687, after a degree of subterfuge on the part of the Trinity Brethren, Turnour agreed to build a completely new lighthouse on the cliff. It was lit for the first time on the 12th September that year. In addition the small light was realigned. The two lights on the Ness continued to mark an alternative channel into the Roads, one favoured by the fishermen. Because of this, these lights became known as the Fishermen's Lights or the Thwart Lights, because any vessel following their line would come in 'thwart the tide'. These were the four lights seen by Defoe in 1722.

2. 1790-1815

During the 18th Century Britain emerged as the world's first industrial nation, a transformation that prompted a dramatic rise in the number of vessels sailing the East Coast. This was good news for Winterton for it meant a welcome increase in salvage work. At the same time a growth in the demand for mackerel and herring, home and abroad, produced a need for more fishing boats and fishermen. The period of the French Wars was therefore one of relative prosperity for the village. All was not plain sailing, however, for Yarmouth became an important naval base and with the Navy came competition for salvage and the iniquitous press gang to add to the interference already meted out by the men of the revenue cruizers in their daily search for smugglers.

The first national population census was taken in 1801. This revealed that at Winterton there were 378 people, divided into 84 families. Given that there were only 54 houses, at least 60 of these families were sharing accommodation. More detail is provided by the 1805 Inclosure documentation.[14] Of the recorded houses, at least 19 were owned by absentee landlords. Residents owned a further 25, for 11 of whom it was their sole dwelling. Of the remainder, two were owned by James Popay, four by Robert Deary and eight by the most prominent Winterton seafarer at this time, Richard Worts. Mention was also made of a public house (The Three Mariners, kept by James King), a brewery, a bakehouse, a coalyard, a warren called Flatgates Farm, and a windmill owned by Henry Bond.

The parish registers reveal that by 1800 a clutch of new surnames had largely displaced those common in the 17th Century. Those that survived from the earlier period included Amis, Brown, Dyble, Hodds and Pile. The newcomers, with approximate dates of arrival, were, Haylett (1690), Kettle (1695), George (1700), Leech (1700), Worts (1720), Sheals (1750), Gunton (1755), Hovell (1755), Smith (1755), Goffin (1760), King (1765), Popay (1770), Bessey (1775), Barnard (1785),

10. The Three Mariners Inn, c1875. The inn staff look on as a group of schoolchildren pose for the camera.

and Symonds (1790). Surnames that arrived shortly thereafter were Soulsby (1805), Larner (1815), Moll (1820), Rogers (1820), Powles (1830), Empson (1835) and Rudd (1835).

The houses they lived in were simple single storey cottages built of beach flints, or brick, with steeply pitched thatched roofs sporting dormer windows. Only the 18th Century Three Mariners and possibly the old rectory were substantial brick buildings with pantiled roofs. The beach flints and reed thatch were local materials and the bricks were mostly made on site. There was, however, another 'local material' and that was ship's timbers, salvaged from the many vessels wrecked on the beach. These were extensively recycled and survive today in the older houses. This made such an impression on Daniel Defoe that he felt compelled to observe; 'I was surprised to see, in all the way from Winterton, that the farmers, and country people had scarce a barn, or a shed, or a stable; nay, not the pales of their yards, and gardens, not a hogsty, not a necessary house, but what was built of old planks, beams, wales and timbers, etc. the wrecks of ships and ruins of mariners', and merchants' fortunes'.[15]

This was still the case in 1880 when a local reporter commented; 'That the good people of Winterton are of an eminently practical turn of mind is sufficiently evidenced by the manner, we were nearly saying the "wholesale" manner, in which they have utilised wreckage for their own private purposes. Not only do we find evidence of the frequent wrecks on this dangerous part of the coast in the "palings" which divide the occupations of many of the residents, but we find the same testimony in the out-buildings, which in many instances have been constructed from the bottoms of boats all thickly pitched to keep out the wet; in the matter too of decoration one's attention is frequently arrested by the figure-head of a ship or the scroll work of her quarter, doing duty in the garden front of a cottage, and peeping out somewhat incongruously from a *parterre* of cabbages, celery or turnips'.[16]

The earliest detailed map of Winterton is dated 1801.[17] The village depicted is spread out along Black Street, with only a smattering of cottages on King Street, Back Road, The Loke, and The Back Path. The church has been omitted, presumably because it was some distance away from the village proper. This raises the question of where exactly was the original Anglo-Saxon village. Usually when a medieval church is some distance away from the main centre it is because the settlement has moved or that the part around the church has fallen into disuse. Both these circumstances may well be the case at Winterton, but the available evidence is inconclusive.

The situation is further complicated by the ever-changing nature of the land to the east and north. The sea-bank looks solid enough today, but this was not always the case. In Hemsby, during the 15th Century, the farm land abutting the sea had the words 'in mare', i.e. in the sea, written against it in the manorial field books, a process of erosion which seems to have continued into the 17th Century.[18] It must be supposed that the adjoining land in Winterton was also suffering the same fate at this time and it is recorded that in 1665, 'by the sea encroaching on the cliffs, (at Winterton) several large bones were found,...'.[19] With the sea reaching the base of the cliff the village must have experienced regular inundations until the 18th Century when marram grass was planted to create the present sea-bank.[20]

The sea-bank also protected the reclaimed marsh to the north, where prior to the late 18th Century lay Flatgates Farm (a name derived from the 'flood gates' on the nearby Hundred Stream). In 1791 the sea burst through this barrier, causing utter devastation as the following account graphically describes. 'Early on the morning of the 3rd February, 1791, Mr. James Bartram, who resided at the Flatgates Farm, Winterton, was aroused by a most unusual commotion, and upon looking from his bedroom window found to his consternation that the sea had broken its bounds and submerged his lands, and in all directions nothing met the eye but a wild surging waste of

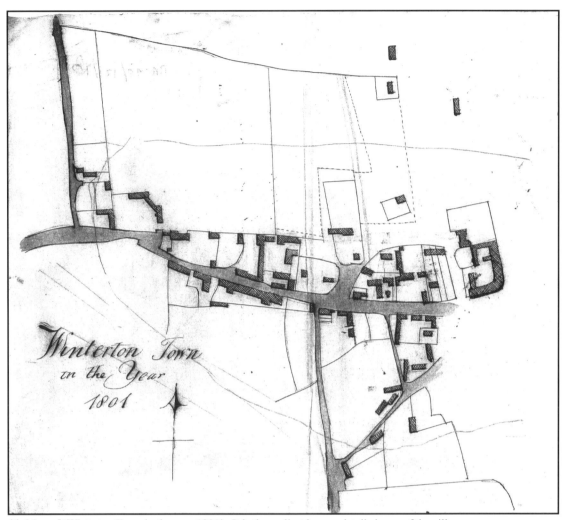

11. Map of 'Winterton Town in the year 1801'. It is the earliest known detailed map of the village.

waters. Arousing his wife and female servant, he ordered them to quit the house at once. Half dressed, the unfortunate people made their way downstairs and escaped by the kitchen window. Almost immediately afterwards the east gable, unable to stand against the rush of water fell in, followed by the roof and opposite gable. Owing to the darkness they feared to move from the place where they were standing, and for two hours remained up to their waists in water. As soon as dawn appeared the farmer, with much difficulty, made his way to the stable and, hastily placing a saddle and bridle upon one of the horses, led it back to the spot where his wife and servant were standing. Having persuaded the women to mount, Mr. Bartram took the bridle in hand and endeavoured to guide the horse through the torrent of water but its force was so great that it swept him away to the end of the garden and he was carried 200 yards further. Ultimately he succeeded in catching hold of a post, and by that means escaped being carried into a ditch which led to Winterton Broad, where inevitable death must have awaited him. In the meantime Mrs. Bartram and the servant in their fright, had fallen from the horse, were carried by the same current to the spot which the farmer had secured a comparatively safe footing, and as they floated within his reach he was enabled to rescue them. For many hours these miserable people suffered the greatest privations and when picked up by a boat were half dead from cold and fright. Mr. Bartram lost the whole of his household goods,

12. Beachmen on the dunes at the stranding of the ketch *Young Fox*, 1910. Left to right, back row; George 'Flower' Smith, John Goffin Jnr., Will Smith, John Goffin, Jimmy Hodds. Front Row; Dennis Olley Leech, Billy Powles, George Larner, Billy King, Josiah Haylett, George 'Plug' Smith, Lew Powles, and George Brown. The man standing on the skyline is Fred Goffin.

many of his cattle perished, and a rabbit warren from which he derived a considerable sum yearly was entirely destroyed'.[21]

The beach was the workplace of the Winterton men and the sea-bank provided a relatively safe place for their 'shuds' and gear. This collection of buildings on both sides of the cart gap resembled a small settlement, perhaps similar to how the village looked in its formative years. It was where the men spent their days when not away deep-sea fishing or 'big boating', as working on merchant ships was termed.

That they worked as merchant seamen and thereby gained experience of the world beyond the narrow confines of the Norfolk coast is demonstrated by the *Betsey* case papers, a ship salvaged by the Winterton beachmen in 1802. In order to show that they were sufficiently experienced to sail merchant ships it was stated that; 'all, or the greater Part of them, were well acquainted with working square-rigged ships particularly Richard Worts, who has been many Years Master of a Brig in the Coal-Trade, Edward Leech, who has sailed in square-rigged Ships in the same Trade, John Amis, who served his Apprenticeship in the same Trade, William Pile, James Fuller, and Isaac Smith, who have all been in the Capacity of Officers in the Greenland Trade (whaling), and James Pile and Benjamin Pile, who have each served an Apprenticeship in large Ships out of Liverpool'...[22]

There were around 70 seafaring men in 1801 and the activity they all took part in was 'longshore fishing. They worked from small clinker built boats and hawked the fish round the adjacent villages or, if large enough, took the catch to Yarmouth. The nets used were braided in the village.

It is difficult to know how many 'longshore boats there were at this time, but as a measure to control smuggling, vessels of a certain size had to be licensed by the Admiralty on the recommendation of the local customs officers. The records of this licensing process mention a number of Winterton boats, several of which do not appear in the contemporary lists of deep-sea fishing vessels.[23] These include the luggers *True Briton*, Samuel George, and the *Persis*, Robert Brown and Robert Deary (1794); the lugsail boats *Dolphin*, Isaac Smith (1796), and the *Lord Duncan*, Robert Leech and Simon Gunton (1797); the open luggers *Speedwell*, Simon Gunton (1805) and the *John & Phoebe*, Samuel George (1805); and the luggers *Benjamin*, Benjamin King and the *Friends* (1808). According to the surveying officer none of these masters/owners, 'have to my knowledge been convicted of smuggling'.

'Longshoring provided a steady income, but the other beach based activity, salvaging, offered the opportunity for spectacular rewards. The men on the beach were used to working together to launch and retrieve their boats, so when there was sufficient salvage work to make it worthwhile, it was logical for them to band together to buy a yawl for the purpose. These groupings became known as beach companies and their members, beachmen.

On the sea-bank the beachmen built a company shed and lookout to enable them to more easily spot vessels in difficulties. Salvage was a valuable business and the right to profit from it, between Winterton Ness and Easton Ness in Suffolk, was vested in the Yarmouth Admiralty Court. It seems, however, that prior to 1790 Winterton's squire, Engle Knights, was running a competing salvage business as an extension of his manorial wreck rights, but that year the court decided enough was enough. In the event an amicable solution was reached, but the real value of this incident lies in the information given about the Winterton beach companies. Reference was made to two companies, the Old Boat's and that of Richard Worts. The membership of the former was just three men, all of whom were around 60 at the time. In 1778 Henry Leech left in his will a tenth share in a boat called the *Pigeon*, which was then lying on Winterton beach, and while it is possible that this was a fishing boat, it is more likely to have been the 'old boat' of 1790. Evidence suggests that this single boat company was formed in the 1760s to carry out salvage work, including the retrieval of anchors.

Worts was described as, 'part owner of several boats, there used for the purpose of taking up

13. The beach, c1910. Note the lifeboat shed, the beach company lookout and the yawl *Band of Hope*.The beach boats include the *Jenny Lind* YH 932.

anchors and cables'.[24] In 1790 the membership of his company stood at 25, mostly men aged between 20 and 35, with Worts, at 52, being the father figure. He probably set up this rival company around 1780, after finishing with the coal trade. He was born in Winterton and on his return from the merchant service became the licensee of The Three Mariners Inn, a position he held until 1794. After resolving the dispute with Knights, the Yarmouth Admiralty Court quickly made Worts a sea reeve, i.e. one of its representatives in Winterton, a move designed to secure the co-operation of the beachmen. It was an office he was to hold until 1820. Between 1790 and 1811 he delivered on behalf of his company135 anchors and other salvaged items to the Court's warehouse. When he died in 1821 he was in possession of 11 houses in Winterton and Yarmouth. He also owned a decked boat and a share in what had become by then the Old Boat's Company. He had been 'Mr. Winterton' for the best part of 40 years, but sadly left no direct descendants. Around 1804 Samuel George emerged as Worts' second in command and ultimate successor, becoming a sea reeve in 1830.

Until the end of the French Wars, Worts' Company was the only one in Winterton. It was the most aggressive and successful within the jurisdiction of the Yarmouth Admiralty Court, having developed the salvage game to a fine art. It was probably this company, which in March 1786 boarded the *Vriende Broder*, adrift between the Haisborough Sand and the shore, after she had struck that notorious sandbank and been abandoned by her master and crew. The beachmen ran her ashore near Waxham and claimed salvage.

In January 1795 the company was involved in something of a sequel to the Knights' case. A large piece of wreckage was salvaged on or near Winterton beach and it was unclear within whose jurisdiction it had been found. A reasonable compromise was reached whereby each party received half the proceeds. Knights' share was £146 16s 8d, from which he no doubt paid the company a

14. Joseph Hume M.P., 1843. The Hume family played a prominent part in village life.

15. Jacob Worts Brown, c1890, great nephew of Richard Worts.

16. A group of beachmen, c1910. Left to right; John George, Ben Popay, Bob King, Arthur King (standing), Charles King, Harry Hovell, and Jimmy King.

proportion. The Admiralty Court received the same amount, from which the company was paid a gratuity of £26 5s.0d.

In 1802 Worts' Company achieved its most spectacular success. On the 5th November the ship *Betsey* sailed from Cronstadt, in Russia, for London with a general cargo. After a two-week voyage, in the darkness of early morning, she struck what proved to be the Haisborough Sand. Thomas Ridley, her master, tried hard to extricate his ship, but at daybreak he hoisted a distress signal. Water was filling her hold and with no obvious sign of help on the way he eventually gave the order to abandon ship.

While this was happening there was a flurry of excitement on the shore. Beachmen on lookout at Winterton, Happisburgh and Caister spotted the casualty and the race was on to secure what would prove to be a very valuable prize. Led on this occasion by Edward Leech, the Winterton men, in a large yawl, reached the vessel first. After patching her up they sailed her into the Yarmouth Roads and later took her into the harbour, but they had had to fend off several rivals, who subsequently turned up at the Admiralty Court as claimants.

As Ridley had abandoned his ship she was declared a derelict, which from the beachmen's point of view was the best possible outcome. The case was heard at the Yarmouth Admiralty Court on the 1st June 1803. As was normal on these occasions the beachmen exaggerated the importance of their work and the master belittled it and them, whilst the other claimants stressed how vital their contributions had been.

After much deliberation the Mayor, as judge in the Court, accepted the Winterton men's claim and awarded them a quarter of the value of the ship and cargo. This was the second highest award ever made in the Yarmouth Admiralty Court. Even allowing for stoppages, the beachmen would have received around £100 each. Understandably dismayed, the ship's owners lodged an appeal with the High Court of Delegates in London and the judgment, given on the 26th April 1804, reduced the award to £2,230. This still left the beachmen with almost £40 each. When it is considered that an agricultural labourer at that time received £20-£25 for a year's toil, the value of the beachmen's eight days work can be fully appreciated.

While the *Betsey* episode demonstrated the beachmen's skill, the *Ney Prove* case of 1810 showed the degree of cunning they were prepared to employ to achieve their ends. On the 21st January 1810, the schooner *Ney Prove* of Copenhagen set sail from Lawkholm for London with a cargo of deals and spars. On the 13th February a branch pilot from Lowestoft went aboard, but that night she struck the Newarp Sand, keeled over, and filled with water. The longboat was immediately launched and all on board abandoned ship, although later it was claimed that they were merely going for help.

Landing at Winterton, the master and the pilot hurried to The Three Mariners to find men to take them back to the schooner. In response the beachmen launched two yawls. The master and pilot boarded one, believing they would be taken to the vessel, but once afloat the yawl headed for Yarmouth. There they had to wait for four hours before being taken out.

In the meantime the crew of the other yawl had boarded the schooner and got her underway. Eventually she was taken into Yarmouth harbour and entered as a derelict by Matthew Haylett. The Court awarded the beachmen £276 5s.0d, clear of all law charges, representing a fifth of the value of the vessel and cargo.

This was a subterfuge the beachmen were to use time after time to secure what they considered to be legitimate salvage, but they rarely shrank from saving life, as most of them knew how it felt to be on the receiving end of trouble at sea. In 1800 the gunbrig *Mastiff* was wrecked on the Cockle Sand and the Winterton men saved 30 of the crew. A grateful Admiralty awarded them 100 guineas, with Abel King and William Pile each receiving 24 guineas for special bravery.

17. A group of beachmen outside Joe Haylett's shed, c1910. Left to right; Joe Haylett, Charlie George, James George, Albert George, Will Smith, Ephraim Hodds, Jimmy Powles, and Walter Dyble.

The *Mastiff* was but one of many naval vessels operating from the Yarmouth Roads during the French Wars. Because of its position Yarmouth became an important naval base and it was from there that Admiral Duncan sailed in 1797 to defeat the Dutch at Camperdown, returning with a large number of prizes. In 1800 Admiral Lord Nelson landed at the jetty after the battle of the Nile and again in 1801, after the battle of Copenhagen. This was good news for the town's businessmen, but not for the Winterton beachmen for the salvage game was open to all and naval vessels represented unwelcome competition. Between 1798 and 1813, 11 naval vessels lodged salvage claims with the Yarmouth Admiralty Court.

Then there was the ever-present threat of the press gang. The Navy had an insatiable demand for experienced seamen. On the 16th July 1803 the Norfolk Chronicle reported that; 'The boats belonging to the men of war lying here assisted by the press gang of this port, impressed a number of seamen who had secreted themselves at Winterton'. The pandemonium that ensued when this determined force had landed on the beach can readily be imagined.

In general terms fishermen were exempt from impressment because fishing was important to the economy. Before the start of a voyage the master of a fishing boat would apply for a certificate of exemption from impress for him and his crew. This would keep them safe at sea, but they could still be taken on land unless they enlisted as Sea Fencibles. Fearing invasion, the Government raised, among other units, a coastal home guard called Sea Fencibles. Carried away with enthusiasm the naval officers in charge raised as many men as they could from the fishing communities, there being no lack of willing recruits, as enlistment provided exemption from impressment.

Between 1803 and 1810 some 67 Winterton men served as Sea Fencibles, exercising for three days a month until 1805 and for one day thereafter. They also manned the signal station with, in 1803, Samuel George and Robert Brown being seconded for that purpose.

Winterton was in the Yarmouth Sea Fencible District, which stretched from Cromer to Covehithe in Suffolk. In 1803 Captain Cobb was sent to take command of the District and a Lieutenant Bamber was stationed at Winterton (other subordinate naval officers held sway at Cromer, Gorleston, and Lowestoft). Bamber was assisted by petty officers drawn from the local recruits. James Symonds was appointed in 1803 and Samuel George in 1804. In 1805 James Popay was given the rank of midshipman, a position he held until the unit was disbanded in 1810.

Service as a Sea Fencible was not very onerous and the men's normal work usually took precedence. In October 1803 some 43 of the 66 on the muster roll did not exercise as they were 'on the fishing'. Similarly in June 1804, only 15 exercised as the others were mackerel fishing. This pattern was the norm throughout the life of this unit.

They also carried out tasks for the Navy. On the 14th April 1804 Thomas Gunton, William Littleboy, and William Hodge (sic) were paid 3s.0d each to escort an impressed man from Winterton to Yarmouth. One suspects that the irony of this duty was not lost on these men.

Safe from impressment very few Winterton men served in Nelson's Navy, but the exemption did not apply to merchant seamen, a distinction which was to be the undoing of Robert Kettle. At the age of 14 he took a berth on a merchantman called the *William* and at the outbreak of the war he was serving aboard the *Hannah*. He probably evaded impressment on a number of occasions, but in 1796 his luck ran out and he was sent aboard the 64-gun man-of-war *Monmouth*, where he began a 17-year stint of uninterrupted naval service.

After being involved in the naval mutiny of May 1797 he and the *Monmouth* joined Admiral Duncan in the Yarmouth Roads within sight, but not reach, of his home. On the 11th October he took part in the battle of Camperdown. The *Monmouth* was in the thick of the fighting, forcing the surrender of the *Delft* and the *Alkmaar*.

18. North Market Road, looking north, c1910. The coal yard was on the left, the newly built Miriam Terrace is on the right.

In 1805 he was transferred to the *Stately*, in 1808 to the *Illustrious*, and in 1813 to the *Bucephalus*, seeing service all over the world. Discharged in 1813 he returned to Winterton and settled down to working from the beach. In 1845 he was living in the cottage now called Ship's Timbers, on the east side of King Street.

The landing of coal was once a common sight on the beach. The squire's coal yard lay on the west side of what is now North Market Road. It was here that coal brought in small colliers was stored, for distribution around the adjacent villages. There was a duty payable on coal and Winterton was one of the designated places where the commodity could be landed. To enable it to be measured for duty purposes the Customs Service appointed men called coal meters. In 1793 Thomas Reeve Fuller, a miller by trade, was appointed to this office in Winterton, on the death of Nathaniel Smith.

Piloting ships into and out of the Roads and beyond was also a service provided by the Winterton beachmen, but illegally, as the Trinity Brethren were responsible for licensing official pilots for this purpose. Most of these pilots worked out of Yarmouth and Lowestoft, but there were a few operating from Winterton. One such man was Valentine John Soulsby. Born in Yarmouth in 1771 he was a ship's master until becoming a pilot in May 1795. On marrying his third wife, Martha Salter, in Winterton in 1807, he moved to the village, but whilst piloting the galliot *Johanna* in the Swin he was drowned, leaving Martha a widow with three young children to support, one of whom, John, was later to achieve prominence in the village.

No survey of beach activity would be complete without reference to smuggling, although there is little official evidence that the Winterton men took part in the illegal trade at this time (nor should there be if they were successful). Given how close they sailed to the wind with their other activities, however, it seems more than likely. Tradition has it that The Three Mariners possessed secret rooms in which contraband was hidden before being taken inland and some of the cottages had double ceilings for the same purpose.

The Customs Service was aware of this possibility and from 1684 riding officers were stationed along the coast. The Winterton Riding Officer patrolled from the Caister Lights to the Waxham Gap and throughout most of the French Wars that man was Lawrence Witchingham. In 1793 he seized 139 gallons of Geneva, but from whom is not recorded. Being an authority figure he was made a sea reeve in 1789 and again between 1792 and 1794. He was replaced in 1811 by John Callow.

The most notorious centre for smuggling at this time was Happisburgh, a landing place which attracted the attention of the revenue cruizers. It was off here that the cruizer *Hunter* foundered on the 13th February 1807, with the loss of all hands. One of these was 25-year-old John Broom, the husband of Mary Ann Broom, whose demise is recorded on a headstone in Winterton Churchyard.

The fortunes of Great Yarmouth were founded on fishing and it was from there that most Winterton men went to find employment in the deep-sea fisheries. Working the Yarmouth boats (and a few of their own) kept them busy for three to four months of the year, split between the mackerel and the herring fisheries. The mackerel fishery started in early May and lasted until the first week in July. Around 30 to 35 boats took part, employing 300 to 350 men, many of them from Winterton. Being highly perishable, the catch was swiftly conveyed in fast sailing carriers to the London market or sold in Norfolk and the adjoining counties.

The herring or home fishing started towards the end of September, when small quantities of fish were caught close to the offshore sandbanks. By the latter part of October they were fully grown and were being caught between Smith's Knoll and the Foreland. This fishery continued until the middle of November with around 150 Yarmouth boats taking part.

It was the town's fish merchants who ran the enterprise, from the purchase and netting of the boats, to curing the catch and exporting the finished product, particularly to the Catholic countries

19. 'Yarmouth Herring boat (lugger) unloading at the Quay', E.W.Cooke, 1829.

20. Edward 'Laurel' Leech, c1850.

of the Mediterranean. They, however, needed experienced seamen to skipper and crew the boats and this is where the Winterton men came into their own. Familiar with the sea from childhood they made excellent skippers.

Before looking at the involvement of these men in detail, it is worth considering the method of catching the fish, for it changed little over the years. John Preston wrote in 1819; 'At the beginning of the season the boats sail off to sea, about ten leagues north-east from this port, in order to meet the shoals, or second part of the first division of herrings, which separate off the north part of Scotland. Being arrived on the fishing-ground in the evening (the proper time for fishing) they shoot out their nets, extending about two thousand two hundred yards of length, and eight in depth, which, by the help of small casks, called bowls, fastened on one side at a distance of thirty of forty yards from each other, are suspended in a perpendicular position beneath the surface of the water. If the quantity of fish caught in one night amount only to a few thousands, they are salted, and the vessels continue on the fishing-ground two or three nights longer, salting the fish as they are caught, till they have obtained a considerable quantity; when they bring them into the roads where they are landed and lodged in the fish-houses'.[25]

The extent to which the Winterton men skippered fishing boats out of Yarmouth at this time can be gleaned from the impressment records. Between 1794 and 1810 nearly 50 Winterton skippers can be identified. Men bearing the surnames Amis, Brown, George, Gunton, Haylett, Hodds, Hovell, Kettle, King, Leech, Olley, Pile, Plummer, Popay, Salter, Sheals, Smith, Symonds and Worts constituted about half the skippers at any given time.

Not content with skippering for others, five luggers belonging to the Yarmouth fishing fleet were wholly Winterton owned. The *Providence*, of 31 tons, was built in 1807, for a consortium of nine, including her skippers James Popay, Matthew Haylett, and James Kettle. The other four luggers were the *Industry* of 31 tons, which is first recorded in 1808, skippered until 1815 by either John Smith or John Brown; the *Rambler*, of 16 tons, recorded from 1809, under skippers Thomas Dible or William Brown; the *Liberty*, of 30 tons, recorded from 1810, skippered by Edward Leech, Edward George, Samuel George or John Plummer, and another *Industry* of 13 tons, mentioned from 1810, skippered by Thomas Brown or J Kettle. All these skippers were almost certainly owners or part owners.

The luggers were kept in Yarmouth harbour, either on the shore or in the docks specially constructed for the purpose. If these owners netted them themselves, their warehouses could be expected to be in the village but, if this was the case, they have left no trace on early maps or amongst the surviving buildings.[26]

3. 1815-1865

Winterton 1845

21. Map of Winterton, 1845.

Victory over the French at Waterloo was followed by a period of social and economic uncertainty, but this had little impact on Winterton where growth continued to be the order of the day. Between 1801 and 1851 the population of the village nearly doubled, before levelling out around the 700 to 750 mark for the remainder of the century, due largely to a migration of people to the burgeoning beach town at Yarmouth and the beach colonies at Caister, California, and Newport.

To cater for this level of growth new houses were built and the housing stock rose from 54 in 1801 to 169 in 1851. Many of these were erected within the confines of the village, but the Tithe Map of 1845 shows how the village had expanded to a shape it was to retain until the end of the 19th Century.

The main areas of new housing were on the northern side of King Street, from just below The Loke, the east side of The Lane, both sides of The Loke, and The Clink, off what is now North Market Road. These houses were generally built in red brick with pantiled roofs, although some of those in The Lane were thatched.

Prompted by social and religious developments and the urge for some to better express their status, a number of significant individual buildings were constructed. In 1830, Robert Porter recorded the melancholy origin of the building, which preceded the Hotel Hermanus. He wrote,… 'about a stones throw to the North of it, (the lighthouse), on the same height, is a handsome, tho small House, called Virginity Cottage most delightfully situated for a summer prospect, not only of the Sea and Shipping, but of the rich lands and woods North, South and West: this house was

22. Hill House, c1910, now the core of the Hotel Hermanus.

built by a single lady, who altho possessed of most of the virtues, had lost Hope, and all the Graces, proving in her person the incorrectness of Popes adage which says "There swims no goose so grey, but soon or late She gets some honest gander for her mate". Miss W…. did not long remain a resident, leaving the place altogether, in 1819 in a fit of disappointment and chagrin, when it was transferred to her friend J B Huntington Esq who sold it with his other property to J Hume Esq and it is now leased to the celebrated Thos Thornhill Esq of Riddlesworth Hall near Thetford'. [27] By 1836 the property was called Hill Cottage and continued to be tenanted until replaced by Hill House in the 1860s.

In the early 1830s the principal landowners were Joseph Hume, who held the Burnley Hall Estate, and the Earl of Winterton, who was also the Lord of the Manor. Around this time the Earl leased his holding to William Womack and on this land Womack built a substantial farmhouse, accessed off Black Street. In 1860 the lease was acquired by Edward Boult and in 1861 the estate was being described as Manor Farm. In 1864 it was called Hall Farm, but in 1868 Boult was described as living in Winterton Hall. The Hall still exists, but it has been converted into flats and lies hidden within a modern housing estate.

In 1821 the Reverend John Nelson, a distant kinsman of Lord Nelson, became the Rector of Winterton. He was clearly unimpressed with the rectory house for he immediately set about building a new one. On the 25th March 1822 he concluded an agreement with Yarmouth builder, John Dyball. The old house was to be demolished and the materials reclaimed for use in the new building. The detailed specification provided for the bricks to be burnt on site and for the brickwork to be given a stone effect colour wash. Nelson borrowed £500 from Queen Anne's Bounty to pay for the work and of him Porter wrote; 'Mr. Nelson is one of those Evangelical Christians who hope to merit Heaven by making Earth a Hell to his Parishioners'. [28]

For years the only inn in the village was The Three Mariners, but in 1830 the Beer Act gained the Royal assent, creating a new type of drinking establishment, the beer house. These were intended to wean people off gin drinking. They were not to open on Sundays and their keepers were only permitted to sell beer and cider. In 1836 Lawrence Rogers was listed as the victualler of The Three Mariners, while Edward Leech, Jnr. and John Juby were described as beer-house keepers. Leech was the local grocer, but by 1845 Juby had become the victualler of what was then called the Fisherman's Arms. This suggests that the Fisherman's Return started life as Juby's beerhouse, a supposition reinforced by the fact that amongst the interesting array of inscriptions scratched into the external brickwork of the inn is one that reads 'JD 1831'. These are probably the initials of the same John Dyball who built the Rectory nine years earlier.

In 1836 an Act of Parliament brought to a close the era of private lighthouses and after paying considerable compensation, the lighthouse built by Sir John Turnour, in 1687, became the property of Trinity House. With so many lights being taken over in this way, that at Winterton had to wait its turn for renewal but, in 1840, a circular towered lighthouse was erected and the old one demolished. This new tower was 62 feet high and its cluster of eleven oil burners and reflectors could throw a beam 17 miles seaward.

Prior to the 19th Century the only place the spiritual needs of the villagers could be met was in the medieval parish church, but this was the age of non-conformity, a simple style of Christian worship, which appealed to a people subject to the fickle whims of the North Sea. In 1811 the house of Ann Kemp was licensed for preaching and in 1812 the Yarmouth Methodist Circuit had seven Winterton members. A Chapel was built in 1814, but it seems that the deed transferring the land had not been properly drawn up and 'the building was lost'. [29]

In 1832 the Primitive Methodists established a presence in the village and in 1843 built a chapel in what is now Old Chapel Road. Set into the gable of this building is a date stone inscribed 'PM CHAPEL 1843 ED LEECH', recording the fact that Edward Leech paid for the building to be

23. The Fisherman's Return, c1910.

24. The Rectory, c1930.

erected. For several generations the Leech family were closely associated with Primitive Methodism, with Dennis Olley Leech being a prominent preacher on the local circuit.

Before 1845 the schooling of the village children was very much a private affair. In 1817 the parish register mentions a schoolmaster, James Thwaites, but whether he was teaching in the village or elsewhere is unclear. White's 1836 Directory states that Mr. Hume supported a school for 30 children, the schoolmaster being Richard Higson. There is no mention of this in the 1841 census, but Amy Larner and Abigail Brown were both recorded as schoolmistresses. In the 1851 and 1861 censuses Amy Larner is described as a schoolmistress living in The Clink, where she ran a day school. Polly Soulsby also ran a school for very young children.

The Norfolk Chronicle of the 2nd July 1842 carried a piece claiming that the village was without daily schools.... 'and the inhabitants (dependent on the contingencies of the sea for their livelihood) (were) too poor to assist in obtaining them.' A sale of ladies' work, 'useful and ornamental,' was to take place on the beach to raise money for the erection of a schoolroom.

In 1845 the National Society for Promoting the Education of the Poor established a National School on land donated by Joseph Hume off the Back Path. George Wilton and his wife Anna were appointed to run the school in accordance with the principles of the established church. Wilton was to stay in the village for the rest of his life, dying there in 1886, at the age of 69. His tenure is commemorated in the following lines of verse;

> 'Old John (George) Wilton is a good old man,
> He try to teach us all he can;
> Reading, writing, 'rithmetic;
> He never forget to give the stick;
> If he do, he'll make us dance;
> Out of England into France,
> Out of France and into Spain,
> Over the hills, and back again'.[30]

The 1851 census provides the first detailed profile of individual villagers. In all 105 men were described, in one way or another, as fishermen most of whom were Winterton born, with the surnames George, Brown, Hodds, Haylett, and Amis being much in evidence. This bears out the statement made by Nall that; 'At this last village (Winterton) they consist of a few large families, the Danish patronymic of George being common, and nicknames, in consequence, rife'. [31]

By contrast, of the 37 farm labourers listed, only 11 were Winterton born, as was only one of the 7 farmers. The shepherd and those engaged in milling, were also outsiders.

This gives the impression that there were two communities living as one, with the 'greenhands', as the fishermen called the farm workers, having more in common with the men of the adjacent inland villages than with their local fishermen, whose way of life was so very different from their own. Having said this, some of the farming lads became fishermen and even founded fishing dynasties, but the converse was rarely the case.

As is to be expected in what was very much a patriarchal society, few women were recorded in the census as having a trade in their own right, most being regarded as either fishermen's wives or daughters. A small number, however, were described as dressmakers and there were two beatsters and two net-makers.

Providing day-to-day services were four shopkeepers, two shoemakers, a butcher, and two publicans. Samuel Larner and his sons ran a building business and there was also a carpenter. Two carriers, Robert Brown and William Flaxman, transported goods and people to and from Yarmouth.

In 1821 Richard Worts bequeathed, 'all my part and share in the Old Companies' boats', showing that by then there was once more two beach companies in Winterton, with his having become the Old Company. The other was the Young Company and evidence from the salvage registers suggests

25. Harvest time, High Barn Farm, c1910. Left to right; Jimmy Bowgin, Jack Took, George Beck, Aaron Rump, Jack Newson, Jimmy Green, Billy Todd, Tom Thirtle, —, Sam Brown, Jonah Greenside, Herbert Hacon, Peter King, Charlie George, and Tom Thirtle Jnr.

it was formed around 1815. By then the village seafaring population had grown to such an extent that those failing to obtain a share in the existing company were able to form one of their own.

With the Old Company secure in its shed to the north of the cart gap, the Young Company beachmen set themselves up on the south side. By 1845, when the tithe map gives the first detailed picture of the beach, the company headquarters buildings are to be seen amidst the sheds of the men of each company.

The rivalry between these two groups touched every aspect of village life, with loyalties within families divided. Tradition has it that if family members were in different companies, care would be taken to only wake their man if one of the companies was launching to a casualty at night.

Each company maintained a fleet of boats, both yawls and gigs, set up on the beach ready to 'larnch'. In the 1840s the Old Company worked the yawls *Paragon* and *Gypsy Queen* and the Young Company the *Young Greyhound* and *Lady Hume*.

There were 40 to 50 members in each, enough to launch and crew two yawls, should the need arise. Their income came from salvage work, servicing shipping, anchor retrieval (called swiping) and taking out pilots. To compete for this work they regularly manned the lookouts and, on a daily basis, made what were termed seeking cruises. Although highly competitive, when it came to the larger salvage jobs they would work together, albeit on terms reflecting which boat had reached the casualty first.

The Yarmouth Admiralty Court was disbanded in 1835, but before then the court record provides a useful insight into the work of the two companies. In 1815 the Swedish brigantine *Aurora*, laden with a cargo of timber, was caught in a gale and abandoned by her master and crew. Later she was found near the Dogger Bank by Christian Shroeder, the master of the ship *St. Beit* of St. Petersburg, and was eventually entered into the Admiralty Court as a derelict. At some stage in the process Schroeder had employed Samuel Box, a Winterton based pilot, together with Robert Deary and the

26. Beachmen and fisher boys alongside the yawl *Band of Hope*, c1905.

27. Charles 'Scuddy' King, 1911.　　　　　　　**28.** Jimmy 'Sorny' Haylett, c1928.

Winterton beachmen to help sail his prize into the Yarmouth Roads. The court awarded the salvors half the value of the net receipts from the sale of the *Aurora's* hull and cargo, amounting to just over £200, but Deary and his men only received 5/70ths of this amount, suggesting that their involvement was purely a matter of providing extra hands. Deary was a member of the Old Company.

On the 22nd October 1824 the brig *Thistle* of Dundee set sail from Riga for Yarmouth with a cargo of hemp. On the 2nd December she struck the Barber Sand (off Caister) and damaged her rudder, before driving over the sandbank and heading in the direction of the Haisborough Sand, where she was eventually abandoned by her master and crew. The Old Company yawl *Lord Wellington*, with William George at the tiller and the Young Company yawl *Friends Adventure*, under James Sutton, worked together to extricate the brig from the sand and bring her into Yarmouth harbour where she was entered as a derelict. For their efforts the two companies shared a tidy £525.

Nearly five years later, in July 1829, the Swedish brigantine *Elizabeth Maria Tonder* left Arendahl in Norway, for Granville in France, with a cargo of timber and deals. Unfortunately, with a strong wind blowing, she struck the Leman and Ower Sand with such force that her rudder was knocked off and, quickly becoming waterlogged, she capsized. Eventually righting herself she was taken in tow by the pilot boat *Nancy*, but then grounded on the Newarp Sand, whereupon her master and crew were taken off.

Almost immediately two yawls from Winterton sped past the pilot boat and, ignoring the onlooking master, their crews boarded the brigantine and got her underway. But such was the violence of the wind and sea she was wrecked on Winterton beach. Her cargo was recovered and the wreck was sold where she lay. The salvors were John Haylett and the crew of the *Greyhound* and John Hodds and the crew of the *Friends Adventure*, both Young Company boats, together with William Goffin and the crew of the *Prince of Wales*, an Old Company boat. As the brigantine was a derelict, the award was half the value of the wreck and cargo, which after the law charges had been deducted, amounted to £100.

In December 1830 there was a carbon copy of the *Betsey* case when the brig *Charlotta* of Stockholm was extricated from the Haisborough Sand. The salvors were the Young Company in the *Greyhound* and *Ino*, and the Old Company in the *Morning Star*. Working together they fended off the competition, including Lieut. Samuel Fielding Harmer, a well-known lifesaver, who felt able to belittle the Winterton men as 'not regular sailors, but beachmen' in order to substantiate his own claim.[32] They in turn cited their sailing experience, but only James Kettle, William George, Robert King, and Joseph Sutton could claim any beyond skippering fishing boats and of those only James Kettle had the experience so extensively cited by the salvors of the *Betsey* in 1803.

By contrast to Harmer's prejudicial opinion, Lieut. Thomas Leigh, the naval officer in charge of the coastguard at Winterton, gave the beachmen a glowing testimonial, adding for good measure details of their heroism as lifesavers. In his evidence to the High Court of Admiralty in 1831, he stated that,… 'several vessels have been wrecked and that upon every such occasion he has found the Winterton men… most willing and desirous of doing all in their power to save the lives of the persons on board such vessels even at the hazard of their own …'[33]

Leigh's mention of lifesaving brings that particular subject into focus. The beachmen went to sea to earn a living, but long before the arrival of specialist lifesaving equipment they saved many sailors in their own boats. Yawls, however, were built for speed, not durability, and the beachmen were well aware of their limitations. They were brave men, but not foolhardy and would not launch if they knew their boats would struggle to survive in the prevailing conditions. This led to the introduction of mortar lines and lifeboats.

The mortar line was developed by Capt. George Manby and was first used on the 12th February 1808, when the seven man crew of the brig *Elizabeth* was rescued after she had grounded in a gale, 150 yards from Yarmouth beach. Mortars were quickly placed along the coast under the control of the Preventive Officers and, in their capable hands, many lives were saved from vessels stranded close to the shore.

A lifeboat was first placed at Winterton in 1822 and was taken over the following year by the Norfolk Association for Saving the Lives of Shipwrecked Mariners. This boat was a 12-oared North Country type, 32 feet long, 10 ½ feet wide and 3 feet deep.

Returning to Lieut. Leigh, he had entered the Navy as a volunteer ordinary seaman in 1803 and was aboard the *Conqueror* at the Battle of Trafalgar two years later. He served throughout the remainder of the Napoleonic Wars, taking part in 10 actions and was four times mentioned in dispatches. When in 1830 he was posted to Winterton to command the coastguard he added lifesaving to his list of achievements.

On the 26th November that year the *Arabella*, a Sunderland collier, became stranded on the Outer Bank at Winterton. Leigh tried to establish a mortar line, but without success and, with the lifeboat being too far away to bring up in time, his eyes alighted on an old beach boat that was scarcely seaworthy. With the beachmen refusing to accompany him he took a mixture of coastguards and Horsey men, and managed to save the whole crew of seven.

This seemed to have impressed the beachmen for on Christmas Eve, when the brig *Henry* of Selby came ashore off the Ness, there was no such reluctance. Leigh recorded what happened next in a letter. 'I hastened… waist deep in snow, to the assistance of a brig… hull under water… all hands lashed to the rigging. As they appeared to be too much exhausted to take advantage of a line thrown over her from a mortar, I directed a lifeboat to be instantly sent for. We put off… and exerted ourselves to the utmost to near the wreck; but a strong flood tide sweeping over us to leeward, and

29. 'All hands to the pumps'. Hauling ashore the lifeboat *Eleanor Brown*, c1910.

a tremendous surf breaking over us, we were compelled to put back; with, however, a determination on my part, if supported, to make another attempt. Fifteen Winterton beachmen and four of my own crew volunteered, and the lifeboat, covered with ice, was again launched. By the greatest possible exertions…we got over the Bank, on which we struck several times with heavy seas breaking over us. Still we persevered, and happily succeeded in closing the wreck, and hearing our shouts feebly returned; but on veering a rope we found the poor fellows incapable of the least exertion. A most dreadful sight then represented itself - the wreck, embedded in a heavy surf, rocking to pieces; the Master suspended from the main shrouds by his heels, a corpse, having bled to death from a wound received on her first striking; the rest of the crew (who had been twelve hours in this perilous situation)…unable to move. Two men… resolutely mounted the rigging, and… handed them to us in the lifeboat, over which several heavy surfs broke, throwing the beachmen into the most alarming confusion. However, we ultimately had the unspeakable satisfaction of safely landing the whole (with exceptions stated) amidst the acclamations of hundreds of spectators'. [34]

Keen to encourage the beachmen, the Norfolk Association were quick to make financial awards. Those who went off in the lifeboat the second time were given a guinea and a half each, while the two men who had boarded, John Soulsby and William George, got an additional guinea. As for the captain and the ship's boy, their bodies were buried in the churchyard, the parish register recording that the captain was Thomas Bollands, aged 35, 'found frozen to death in the shrouds' and the boy, 15 year old John Chapman.

In January 1831 Lieut. Leigh and William George were together again in a yawl, saving the crew of seven from the *Vulcan*, wrecked near Winterton. Two years later, in March 1833, the barque *Crawford* from Hamburg to London, with 40 horses, ran aground on the Haisborough Sand, and began to sink. Leigh put off in the lifeboat and rescued 16 men, who ironically were Palling beachmen who had boarded her and become stranded.

Leigh's sterling work as a lifesaver earned him promotion to Commander in 1835, the same

30. The beach company lookout, c1920. It was demolished in 1922.

year he saved three of the crew of the collier brig *Blackbird*, like the *Henry* stranded on a shoal off the Ness. For his exploits he was awarded the National Shipwreck Institution's gold medal, gold boat and silver medal.

Although successfully used by Leigh the first lifeboat was not very popular with the beachmen, and in the Northumberland Report of 1851 it was noted that at Winterton; 'No one will go afloat in the life-boat. Rockets have burst, and lines broken here'.[35] In 1858 she gave way to a 30 foot self-righter, which in turn was replaced three years later by a 32 foot Norfolk and Suffolk type boat, which in 1867 was given the name *Ann Maria*.

The mortar and rocket line apparatus continued to be used by the coastguards to try to effect rescues, but their efforts were not always trusted. In November 1838 the brig *Wonder*, from Hamburg to London, grounded outside the Outer Bank at Winterton. Chief Coastguard, Lieut. Hains, succeeded in establishing four lines from the mortar and also a rocket line, but the crew would not venture to save themselves and all perished. The wreck was sold on the beach where she lay. Nine years later the same thing happened when Chief Boatman-in-Charge Robert Lugar was informed that a vessel had grounded two miles to the north of the village. He immediately sent word to local farmer, William Womack, who despatched horses and men to take the mortar to the spot. Lugar managed to secure two lines to the vessel, but the crew continued to cling to the rigging until both masts fell and they also perished.

While the coastguards actively tried to save lives their primary purpose remained the prevention of smuggling. The end of the Napoleonic Wars saw a strengthening of both the land and seaborne branches of the preventive service, assisted by the fact that the Navy now had men and ships to deploy. In 1822 the service was reorganised to improve efficiency, with the new force being called, for the first time, the Coastguard. This term encompassed the land-based preventive water-guard, the revenue cruizers, and the riding officers, although the latter were greatly reduced, with the one at Winterton being withdrawn once the preventive station was operational.

A preventive station was established at Winterton in 1817 and a combined watch house and boathouse was built to the south of the cart gap, in 1819. The complement of this station was a chief officer, a chief boatman, two commissioned boatmen, and four ordinary boatmen. The first

Chief Officer of Coastguards was Lieut. Robert Bates Matthews. He was followed by a succession of nine naval lieutenants, until Robert Lugar arrived from Yarmouth in 1844 as Chief Boatman-in-Charge, a position he held until replaced by John Bungard in 1856.

The watchhouse contained a lookout, a gear store, and a place to keep the mortar and rocket apparatus. It was also the home of the chief officer. In 1851 Robert Lugar was living in this exposed position with his wife and six children. The remainder of the coastguards were billeted around the village until the late 1840s, when six cottages were built for them within the old brewery complex. These became known as the Barrack Yard. In the 1860s a terrace of eight houses off King Street replaced them.

Coastguards, especially the chief officers, were rarely allowed to stay at one station long, for this could lead to a level of familiarity, which could render them ineffective in their pursuit of smugglers. Fraternisation, however, did inevitably take place. Between 1840 and 1900 five coastguards married in the parish church, as did the daughters of six others. One of these coastguards, however, was Winterton born William Goffin, who joined the service in 1847 and returned to his home village the following year to wed Elsie King. He ended his working days at the Snettisham coastguard station, in West Norfolk.

A reminder of why the coastguards were stationed at Winterton is provided by the Norwich Mercury of the 10th March 1838. The report reads: 'On Thursday last the Hope of Flushing was seized by Lieut. Hains, R.N. chief officer of the coast guard, Winterton, having on board one half anker of foreign spirits in an illegal cask, also 3 foreigners, she was brought into this (Yarmouth) harbour today. A Boat was likewise seized at break of day on the beach by this officer with 112 half-ankers of foreign spirits, and 99 bales of tobacco which was lodged in the custom house'.

No Winterton men were mentioned, but anecdotal evidence of their possible involvement with smuggling at this time is provided by the recollections of Elizabeth, the daughter of John Soulsby,

31. Coastguards with the rocket cart outside the rocket shed, c1910.

who kept The Three Mariners in the 1850s. He was the most prominent beachman of his day, and was reputed to be the strongest man in East Norfolk. Late in life Elizabeth recalled an occasion when, as a child, she had gone down to the beach with her Aunt Chris (Christiana Kettle, nee King), who had a lantern concealed under her cloak. Standing on the seaward side of one of the many beach boats, Aunt Chris had signalled to a vessel at sea, knowing she would get away with it because the coastguard would not take notice of a woman and child strolling on the beach.

She also related the tale of another relative who lived in a cottage, which had a double ceiling for concealing contraband, the space between being accessed via a hidden panel. On one occasion, when the hiding place was full, a party of coastguards had arrived from Yarmouth and asked the whereabouts of the cottage. Predictably the men were sent on a wild goose chase, giving the smugglers time to remove their goods, all except, that is, for one keg. The relative stood this on the hearthrug and, after taking up her knitting, sat down so that her skirts concealed the incriminating evidence. Moments later the coastguards arrived and, after making a show of searching the whole cottage, went to the hiding place, but finding nothing there they left with a barrage of colourful language ringing in their ears.

With the closure of the Yarmouth Admiralty Court in 1835, the comprehensive record of the beachmen's salvage work disappears, but the county newspapers continued to report significant cases. In November 1856 the brig *Adder*, from Hamburg for Liverpool and South America, came ashore on Winterton beach. Her cargo of general merchandise was removed and under an agreement for £300 the beachmen extricated the brig and took her into Yarmouth harbour.

In May 1858 there was an adjudication hearing concerning services rendered to the schooner *Catherine Maria* of Barth, with a cargo of wheat to the value of £1,100. Having spotted that the

32. The coastguard watch house with Hill House in the background, c1900.

32

33. William and Elsie Goffin, c1890. He was a coast-guard at Snettisham.

34. Caroline Brown nee King, wife of Maurice, c1900.

vessel was flying a flag for assistance, John Soulsby and the Old Company immediately launched the yawl *Star*, with a crew of 10 and a gatway pilot, Winterton man Benjamin King. On arrival the master said that he wanted someone to take the schooner to London, so King was left on board and the yawl set a course for home. Quickly discovering that the schooner had struck a sandbank and had two feet of water in her hold, King refused to pilot her and signalled for the beachmen to return to work the pumps. By the time they reached the harbour she was almost sinking. The *Emperor* steam-tug was engaged and the schooner was beached in the harbour. Soulsby and the Old Company were awarded £220 for their efforts, with the costs being divided between the two parties.

Probably the last Young Company salvage job took place on the 18th August 1868, when Robert Warnes and the Company rendered services to the brig *Wikenger*, from Christiania, for London with deals. Seeing that she was signalling for assistance, a yawl was launched and on reaching the brig, the master said he wanted to be taken into the Roads. Warnes asked for £150 but the Captain was only willing to pay £15. This was accepted as a pilotage fee, but when Warnes found that some of the crew were sick and that men were needed to work the vessel, he told the Captain more would have to be paid. After taking her safely into the Roads the beachmen were awarded £45 and costs.

The work of the beachmen was hard and dangerous, but the various marine regattas offered them the opportunity to pit their wits against their rivals in less desperate circumstances. Regattas were held at Yarmouth between 1830 and 1910 and the Winterton men regularly took part. They were fairly low-key affairs until the coming of the railways in the mid 1840s, which brought large numbers of day-trippers, not so much to view the racing, but to have a good time on the beach, where other entertainments abounded. This attitude was not surprising for the events at sea were slow and very difficult to understand.

There were usually six to eight matches at each regatta, the first nearly always being a yacht race. Yawl races followed and were generally considered to be the most interesting of the day, as they were keenly contested. Both races were sailed around a double triangular course of some six to eight miles, making a total distance of 20 miles in all. The faster yawls could cover the distance in three hours, but some would take as long as five. The prize money, shared between the first, second, and third boats, usually amounted to between £20 and £30. The races were sailed on a handicap basis, an allowance of 30 seconds per foot being made.

The pattern of the yawl races closely mirrored the fortunes of the beach companies. Until 1843 the newspapers only reported the placed boats and these all came from the Yarmouth companies. The first Winterton yawl to be featured was the Old Company's *Morning Star*, unplaced in the 1844 regatta. She competed until 1848, but only achieved a fourth place. The Young Company's *Young Greyhound* put in an appearance in 1846 and again in 1850, but fared no better, being unplaced on both occasions. Between 1849 and 1865 the Old Company's *Gypsy Queen* took part, achieving the village's first victory in 1863, together with two second and two third places. Over the same period the Young Company's *Lady Hume* achieved a second and a third. From 1866 to 1876 the *Electra* and the *Band of Hope* competed, with the former achieving an excellent three wins, a second and a third in six races. The *Band of Hope* was third twice.

There followed a nine year gap when no yawl races were held at Yarmouth, a reflection of the low ebb that the beach companies had reached, but on their resumption in 1886 the Winterton Company's yawls *Paragon* and the two *Bands of Hope* won three between them before the last yawl race in 1907.

Matches were also arranged for beach company gigs and coastguard boats. On six occasions lifeboats were also put through their paces. In 1845 and 1851 the Winterton lifeboat took part, but on the latter occasion the intense rivalry that existed between the various crews got out of hand, as related in the following newspaper report; '…In accordance with this spirit of jealous competition, a naval battle took place, during the trial with sails – between the Winterton boat and another, which no doubt was settled by a renewal of the contest when the labours of the day were over. The

35. The village from the sea-bank, c1950.

36. The Lane, looking south, c1900.

Winterton boat is small, and on the occasion in question, upon the signal to hoist sail being given, instead of making away she fell off with the tide, as did also her companion, for the time. Presently, however, her competitor recovered, and the sturdy Winterton boat, in order to get herself into wind, attached herself to the gaff of her fortunate sister, and made the better chances her own. This was resented, oars were unshipped and a furious battle commenced, until, in fact, the Winterton boat was beaten away…'[36] The Winterton lifeboat played no further part in the exercises.

By this time the Winterton beachmen were not only competing with each other they were having to contend with their relatives and former friends, who had migrated to the newly established beach colonies from Newport to Yarmouth. This migration had its roots in rapid population growth and the expansion of the Yarmouth fishing industry. Yarmouth was the main attraction, it seeming senseless to many to keep making the 18 mile round trip to and from the port. Contrary to what might be supposed, it was mainly experienced men who moved, and many of them became prominent in the town's fishing industry. On leaving Winterton they sold their company shares and bought into the Yarmouth companies. Of the beachmen, fishermen and fish merchants recorded in the 1851 Yarmouth census, 62 were Yarmouth born, whereas 38 were of Winterton origin, spread throughout the five Yarmouth beach companies.

At the same time others were migrating to Caister where they were to dominate the beach community there. The first man to do so was Robert George, who had the Ship Inn built in 1815. It was the first building to be erected in the Caister beach village. His influence was probably instrumental in bringing in other Winterton men; Samuel George, Edward George. and John George, between 1810 and 1820; Thomas George, between 1820 and 1830; William George, Benjamin Hodds, and John Haylett, between 1830 and 1840; and William Hodds, Samuel Symonds, John and William Plummer, and Humphrey Dyble between 1840 and 1850.

The next decade witnessed a further influx of Winterton men, who all but took over the Caister beach company. These included Isaiah Haylett, Aaron King, Benjamin Kettle, Jacob George, Philip George, John George, and the most famous of them all Old Jimmy Haylett.

In the 1840s other migrants founded a beach colony at Newport and, a decade later, one at California. In addition a significant number moved north to Sea Palling. In each case the Winterton men took with them their expertise and either started a new beach company or improved on an existing one. By the 1860s, while Winterton still retained its two original companies, men born in the village were prominent in all those from Yarmouth to Sea Palling and the names George, Haylett, Hodds, and Brown were common to them all.

There was a significant migration to other port towns, the most extensive being that to Goole, where at least 22 inter-related Winterton adults became established during the latter part of the 19th Century.[37] One individual migrant is also worthy of notice and that is Martha Rudd. She was born in Winterton in 1845 and became the mistress of Wilkie Collins, the author of *The Moonstone* and *The Woman in White*. He met her in 1864, whilst on a visit to the Yarmouth area, and she moved to live with him in London, where they had three children.[38]

The life led by the Winterton seafarers was a precarious one, with their income largely dependent on chance. If the fishing was poor and salvage work scarce, there would be real hardship in the village. It has already been noted that the people were too poor to provide a school and in 1845 William White wrote that; '…in winter (the fishermen) are subject to much privation; machinery having robbed them and their families of their former employment in braiding fishing nets'.[39]

Families tended to look after their own, but sometimes this was not possible. In 1857 the Winterton Provident Friendly Society was formed to help those who, owing to sickness or accident, found themselves in financial difficulties. There were 32 founder members headed by Abel King. Within 10 years that number had trebled. The printed rules of the Society were carefully framed to

37. Beachmen alongside the surf lifeboat *Edward Birkbeck*, c1910. Left to right; Ben Bessey, —-, —-, Charlie Leech, Jimmy Annison, Robert Powles, Walter Powles, Jimmy Haylett, Robert George, John Chaney, Charlie Larner, George Haylett, Charlie Bessey, Walter Kettle, Jeffrey Moll, Jimmy Moll (coxswain), —-, and Jack Watson.

38. Old Jimmy Haylett of 'Never Turn Back' fame, c1905. He migrated to Caister at the age of 27.

39. Philip George, Caister lifeboat coxswain, c1875. He migrated to Caister at the age of 22.

prevent fraud, for example, anyone 'on the club' was expected to be indoors at dusk and to remain there until daylight the next day, no doubt to aid a speedy recovery. The society was active for over a hundred years before its closure in 1970.

Throughout this period the hundred or so Winterton fishermen continued to be employed in the Spring mackerel fishery and the Autumn herring fishery, many of them skippering the Yarmouth boats, as confirmed by Nall, who commented that; 'Almost all the beachmen in these villages (Winterton, Caister, California and Newport) are either masters or mates of herring boats'.[40]

Deep-sea fishing boat owning was a different matter. By 1835 only the *Providence* had survived from the earlier period, still owned by a Winterton consortium, but her registration was cancelled in 1840.

In 1845 fish merchant, William Juby, bought the newly built *William Tell* and ran her until 1852, when failure to pay back a loan, resulted in her being sold to Ben Hodds, a Winterton migrant to Caister. In 1848 John Amis, in partnership with Hemsby man, William Bushell, bought the *Hope* and ran her until 1852, when he acquired Bushell's share and migrated to Yarmouth.

The only other Winterton men to venture into boat ownership at this time were the George brothers, Aaron, Ambrose, and Robert. In 1857 they bought the new lugger *Caroline*, but unfortunately she was lost on the Scroby Sands in 1859. By that time Aaron, nicknamed 'Driver', was described as of Gorleston, where in 1888 he was drowned when the lifeboat *Refuge* capsized.

It was not only the working of a yawl or a lifeboat that could result in an early death. On the 28th May 1860 a calamity of such proportions struck the fishermen that it is still remembered along the East Coast as the May Gale Disaster. A severe gale, blowing from the north-west, created havoc across the North Sea. Many merchant ships were driven ashore or onto the sandbanks, with much loss of life. Worse for Winterton, the mackerel fleet was caught in the open sea and many luggers were lost with all hands. Other men were washed overboard from those that managed to limp into port.

As usual with these disasters, a relief fund was quickly set up for the dependants of those drowned and its records list 21 boats from which 179 men were lost, together with a further 15 from the boats that survived. This left 76 widows and 191 fatherless children, not to mention many grieving parents. Of the £10,410 raised, 30% was paid to Yarmouth dependants and 18% to those in Winterton. This was the second highest amount suggesting that the village lost a large number of men.[41] No comprehensive list exists, but the records of the Provident Society reveal that Robert Dyble, George Flaxman, Isaac George, George Hodds, and James Smith were drowned and to these can be added the names of William Brown and Benjamin King, whose deaths are recorded in the churchyard. Such catastrophes happened all too frequently, but none had more impact on Winterton than the May Gale.

4. 1865-1914

40. Beach Road, looking east, c1900.

Towards the end of the 1860s the Winterton beach companies were reorganised and involvement in the Yarmouth deep-sea fisheries entered a new phase. These events mark the start of another 50-year period in the story of Winterton, one that was to last until the outbreak of the First World War. There were, of course, the usual good times and bad, which characterised the lives of those who depended on the vagaries the sea, and it is with an event organised to help the villagers in their hour of need that this section starts.

On Tuesday the 10th August 1880 several thousand excited people descended on Winterton to witness the first marine regatta to take place there. Many of them arrived at Hemsby station and either walked the last mile or so by road or along the beach, or took advantage of the many horse drawn conveyances pressed into service for the purpose.

With the encouragement of Mrs. Hume, a committee of local notables had raised sufficient funds to offer prizes for a variety of matches to be competed for by the local fishermen and the scene was set for a memorable day.

The reporter of the Yarmouth Independent described in full the jollities that took place, but he also highlighted the serious nature of the event. 'It must not be forgotten', he wrote, 'that the *raison d'etre*… was not so much the providing an afternoons pleasurable recreation as the affording a little encouragement to the beachmen at this small fishing station. It was known that the last winter was anything but a favourable one for the boatmen, who depend mainly for their livelihood on the salvage services they are enabled to render to vessels in distress, and for which work they are obliged to keep up not only a valuable fleet of boats, but a staff of men experienced in their working, and accustomed to put off in all weathers, and often at great personal risk. The dearth of salvage employment and the subsequent failure of the fisheries usually prosecuted by the Winterton beachmen, led to a desire on the part of some of the more influential inhabitants of the parish to

41. The parish church, c1875, showing the roof line before the restoration of 1877/8. On the rear of the original photo is written 'Winterton Church Amphibian Harvest'.

consider how best they could afford encouragement to the crews, and at the same time testify their sense of the patience displayed by the men under circumstances at once trying and depressing'.[42]

Much effort had gone into making the village look attractive and welcoming to its visitors. Bunting was everywhere, with the most notable displays adorning the lighthouse, beachmen's shed and the coastguard station. James King of The Three Mariners and Jimmy Waite of the Fisherman's Return made sure their cellars were full and the latter erected a large refreshment tent on the beach where 'viands of excellent quality were obtainable'. The band of the 2nd Norfolk Rifles provided most of the musical accompaniment and taking advantage of the crowds on the beach were eager vendors, photographers, and entertainers.

Unfortunately the same reporter felt the village left a lot to be desired. 'To the visitor of fastidious, to say nothing of asthetic tastes, we would not at any time of the year commend a visit to Winterton, as their feelings would doubtless be shocked at many things that to the local mind are but every-day matters, and scarcely worth consideration. What did for their forefathers is a matter of equal content to the residents of to-day, and therefore the spirit of improvement which has set in so strongly in some places, may be said to have scarcely reached so far east as Winterton. Not that the parish has been wholly neglected, far from it, the newly restored church would at once dispel that idea; but the first impression that would probably be made in the mind of the visitor is not so much what has been done, as what remains to be done. Evidently there is no need of a School Board, that blessing having already been accorded the parish, but to the pedestrian on Tuesday, whose avocations either for pleasure or business led him to traverse the main thoroughfare, or shall we be polite and say "High" Street of Winterton, there appeared urgent need of an energetic board of works. The roads, it is no use disguising the fact, are not of a nature to impress one greatly with the resources of the parish, and one is puzzled in noting the ingenuity displayed in many other directions, that something more has not been done to facilitate locomotion'. He did, however, concede that; 'the place has much to be said in its favour as a health-giving resort. We question if at any point on the coast is there a finer beach or a more bracing atmosphere than is to be found at Winterton, or a place where a stroll over its breezy hills could more effectually sharpen the appetite'.[43]

At 12.30 prompt the starting gun for the opening race sounded and seven first class brown-sailed beach boats set off to complete three laps round a double triangular course. Eventually, after a hard fought contest, the *Donald* (W George) took the £5 first prize, the *Providence* (G Dyball) took £2 for second, and the *William and Ann* (S Rogers) £1 for third. Those unplaced were the *Alice* (J Waite), the *John Able* (J King), the *John Frederick* (J Goffin) and the *Rover* (J Dyball).

The next race, for second-class beach boats, was won by the *Troas* (J King), with the *Birkbeck* (M Browne) second and the *HRH* (W Hodds) third. Unplaced were the *Eva Ellen* (W Hodds) and the *Tally Ho* (J Browne). The third race was for small boats sailing twice round the course. This was won by the *Young Recruit* (D Leech) followed by the *Fly* (J King) and the *Shah* (Dyball). Also taking part were the *Emma* (J Waite) and the *Lily* (J Dyball).

After this a great many people 'including ladies', were taken out for a cruise in the yawl *Paragon* and one of the boats from the first race. Later events included a rowing match, a demonstration of the life-saving apparatus and the obligatory duck hunt, which concluded the activities at sea.

The day was a great success, especially for the beachmen who, in addition to making some welcome cash, were able to show off their 'longshore fishing fleet. In all 17 beach boats were named requiring up to 50 men to crew them, a reminder of just how important 'longshoring' was to the village economy.

The nature of this work and the type of fish caught can be gleaned from a number of brief notices in the Yarmouth Independent. In April 1874 it was reported that the 'longshoring was good and

42. 'Longshore boats, c1910. The yawl *Band of Hope* is in the background.

43. Landing mackerel from the 'longshore boat *Kate* YH5, c1905. Left to right; Walter Dyble (boat's owner), William Dyble (his brother), and Albert (William's son).

that there had been an addition to the fleet, a boat owned by John, Robert, and Frederick Goffin. In June that year fishing for mackerel was poor, the best catch being 50 fish caught by Matthew Dyble, in the *Providence*. Some boats had been trawling, with John Brown in the *Mermaid* catching a 'double of soles'. Later in the year it was reported that he had caught a large piece of amber.

In January 1875 the boats were busy long-lining for codling, with large numbers being taken. The newspaper was pleased to report that, 'Our old friend, Samuel Haylett, the oldest fisherman in the place, 84 years, and of course past fishing, continues to make himself heard amongst us'[44] Mention was also made of Edward Fawcett, 'who was with Sir John Ross in his memorable expedition in search of Sir John Franklin at the frozen regions of the north,… The contrast between the present and the time of his Arctic experiences, must be great indeed, but no doubt even cod fishing at Winterton is preferable to being frozen up three years, hundreds of miles from home'.[45] In May the boats had started earlier than usual and one belonging to Matthew Dyble had landed 250 mackerel, selling at £2 a hundred.

In late April 1879 some of the boats were making a success of shrimping and in May the first salmon were caught by John Goffin and Matthew Dyble, the former landing 22, the latter 11. Later that year trawling was poor, there being too few fish to catch. The same was true of shrimp and mackerel fishing. The 'oldest inhabitant' had never known a season like it. Fishing was so bad that many of the fishermen had to resort to haymaking to put food on the table, but in October 'longshoring for herring partly saved the day, with some boats catching as many as 2,000 fish.

The 'longshore fishing industry of Winterton was very much a microcosm of the Yarmouth based deep sea fishing, with most of the Winterton smack-owners also owning beach boats from which they fished. These boats were clinker built and sported lug sails. In the period before the First World War they cost £1 a foot. More often than not they were named after a family member or members. In the main the men who sailed them owned them, but some had more than one and hired them to others on a share basis. Such a man was Wilks Larner who owned five. In 1902, when returning from Yarmouth, having taken a large catch there, his boat, the *William*, struck the submerged piles of the Caister sewer outfall and he and his crew were forced to jump overboard. Fortunately all four men reached the shore safely, but the boat sank.

The 'longshoremen's tackle and nets were stored and maintained in sheds on the dunes. Nets were also braided there and in the village. In June 1908 a new communal tanning copper was built alongside the track to the beach. Here nets were steeped in preservative before being spread on the dunes to dry and woe betide any boy who had the audacity to scamper across them!

Around 1868 the two beach companies became one. Tradition has it that William Burnley Hume persuaded the beachmen to end their rivalry and, to seal the deal, he presented them with their own private lifeboat, the *Minnie Hume*, named after his adopted daughter. The Norwich Mercury provides the background to this event. 'Hitherto both Winterton and Palling have been without a lifeboat fit to go off to the Haisborough Sands in bad weather, and the California and Caister lifeboats have had the more to do on that account, but this year each of these stations, so much nearer the Hasboro Sands than these are, have been presented with a large lifeboat, and now competition between the beach companies hereabouts will be all the greater, and success will not so much depend upon the possession of a good boat now, as upon the bravery and vigilance of the crews that man them'.[46]

It is somewhat surprising that the beachmen accepted this boat, for she was formerly the Gorleston lifeboat *Rescuer*, which had capsized in 1866 and again in 1867 with the loss of 18 boatmen. In 1875 it was said that the *Minnie Hume* had been responsible for saving upwards of 40 lives. She continued in service until at least 1893 when she was towed out to the Haisborough Sand by a steam-tug in order to rescue a large number of people from the stranded barque *Ruby*.

In reality, the underlying cause of the amalgamation was the need for both companies to renew their boats and, with the salvage work shrinking, the finance for this was not easy to find. The Old

44. The double lifeboat house, c1910.

45. The Beach Company shed and lookout, c1915.

Company's yawl *Gypsy Queen* is not mentioned after 1865 and its yawl *Paragon* was broken up in 1868. Similarly the Young Company's yawl *Lady Hume* had her registry cancelled in 1864 and the *Young Greyhound* was broken up in 1869. These yawls were replaced by the *Electra*, the *Band of Hope*, and the *Paragon*. The *Electra* is not mentioned after 1876 and around the turn of the century a severe gale swept the *Paragon* and the *Band of Hope* onto the dunes, rendering them unseaworthy. They were replaced by a new *Band of Hope*, the last in a long line of Winterton yawls.

The combined company had around 90 members and ran its affairs from a new shed and lookout to the north of the cart gap. Renewed in this way there must have been a degree of optimism, but the factors, which would eventually cause the closure of the beach companies, continued to impact. Success in the salvage business depended on an ever shifting sandbank system, the dependence on sail power, and a beach company monopoly of salvage work. Over the years buoys and lighthouses made it safer to negotiate the sandbanks and the introduction of steam power and iron ships greatly reduced the number of casualties. In addition, those that did occur often needed more help than the beachmen could muster, and the steam-tugs could do the easier work for a fraction of the price.

By the 1870s these changes had devastated the town companies, but the village companies were better able to cope and even learned to work with the steam-tugs. Apart from slack periods, such as the one that prompted the regatta of 1880, the Winterton beachmen continued to be reasonably successful.

In 1871 the brigantine *Scud*, of Scarborough, from Hartlepool bound for London, with railway iron, sprung a leak when nearing the Cockle Sand and the 20-man crew of the yawl *Paragon*, together with the crew of the smack *Myrtle*, were awarded £160 for helping her into Yarmouth harbour.

In 1879 the barque *Lyra* of Shoreham, from Shields bound for Cape de Verde, with coal, came ashore on Horsey beach. The Winterton beachmen were employed to salvage her for £500. They threw overboard 60 tons of cargo and laid out an anchor, but with this being unsuccessful they engaged a steam-tug for £25, whereupon the *Lyra* was towed into the Yarmouth Roads.

Such jobs continued at a steady rate and in 1890, two large payments enabled the beachmen to build a new brick shed and a timber lookout and put their boats in order. In March that year the *SS. Circassian Prince*, of Newcastle, grounded on the Haisborough Sand and was salvaged by a consortium consisting of the Winterton beachmen in the lifeboat *Margaret* and yawl *Band of Hope*, the Sea Palling beachmen in the lifeboat *British Workman* and the yawl *Dart*, and the steam-tugs *Yare*, *Gleaner*, *Tom Perry*, and *Star*. The award for getting her off was £3,500, with half going to the steam-tugs. Of the remainder, 5/9ths was given to the Winterton men and 4/9ths to those from Sea Palling.

In May the *SS. Golden Horn* of West Hartlepool, bound from Shields to Savona, with coal, ran aground on the Hammonds Knoll and was abandoned by her crew. Once again a large consortium of salvors saved the day and was awarded £2,600 for their efforts. This time they comprised William Hodds and 79 beachmen in the yawls *Paragon* and *Band of Hope* and the lifeboat *Margaret*, the crew of the Gorleston lifeboat *Elizabeth Simpson*, and the steam-tugs *Yare*, *Express*, and *Star*, belonging to the Great Yarmouth Steam-tug Company Ltd., the one the Winterton men worked with on a regular basis. The steam-tug *Harwich* was also involved.

The Journal of John Hopknee King provides details of the money doled out to the beachmen in the early years of the 20th Century.[47] In 1900 they each received £5.13s.6d for salvaging the *SS. Syble* and, in 1902, £2.11s.6d for services to the barque *Chili*, which had become a total wreck on Winterton beach. The insurance company paid the beachmen £1.17s.6d per standard to unload her cargo of timber and in March the wreck itself was sold by auction to the local squire, George Beck, for £190. The cargo was also auctioned, fetching £2,230. Beck employed the beachmen to break

46. Group of men and lads on the beach, c1910.

47. The barque *Chili* ashore on Winterton beach, 1902. The hulk was bought by George Beck for £190.

up the wreck, a task that was not completed until January 1903. It is said that he got more for the copper off her bottom than he had paid for the whole wreck. Many of the fishermen did not go to sea that year as they could make more money working on the wreck.

Later in 1902 £2.2s.0d was doled out for the *SS. Teal* and in 1903 a handsome £14.7s.0d for the *SS. Martello*. In 1906 the *SS. Bushmills* yielded £2.2s.4d per man and in 1910 the ketch *Young Fox* produced £1.3s.6d. The following year £3.5s.0d was paid for the *SS. Lincoln*.

Newspaper reports are useful in giving the facts of these cases and something of the drama involved, but it is from eyewitness accounts that the local flavour can best be gleaned. In June 1904 the *SS. Osprey* ran ashore on Winterton beach after being in a collision. The crew of 36 was rescued by the *Edward Birkbeck* lifeboat and the wreck was eventually sold by auction for £60. The beach was strewn with goods, more than anyone had ever seen before. There were cases of whiskey, picture books, tins of biscuits, cases of earthenware, glazed paper, and much more. Valentine Larner and his brother Spindle went down to the beach and found some staunch chapel men with a case of bottles they had just pulled from the sea. The men told them that the bottles contained ketchup, so they thought they would have a case for themselves. Pulling one out they discovered, to their surprise, that the bottles contained whiskey. 'We drank some, buried nine bottles in the hills, and went and told our mother. She said we should tell the coastguard but we had already broached them'.

In January 1900 the barque *Theodor* came ashore north of the gap. She was supposed to be bound for the USA with toys, but actually had a cargo of raw spirit, 'strike me hot in Jimmy Johns'. This windfall was quickly taken away and hidden around the village. Many of the beachmen stayed with the wreck for days until the spirit was all gone.

Looking for goods washed up on the beach was called 'pawking', something practised by everyone in the village. Ambrose George was said to have found a portmanteau containing enough money to have a bungalow built. It is probably this activity that earned the Winterton people the nickname Chitterunners (or Chittlerunners), from the birds that run behind a receding wave to see what 'chittle' (scraps) they can find.[48]

The lifeboat service boards in the parish church reveal that 436 people were rescued between 1858 and 1924. This is an impressive record. The surf lifeboat *Ann Maria* was the only RNLI boat at Winterton until 1879, when the heavier *Husband* was transferred from the Corton Station. Shortly before this the *Ann Maria* was renamed the *Edward Birkbeck*. In 1896 she was replaced by a new boat of the same name. By then the *Husband* had been replaced by the *Margaret*, which, in 1899, gave way to another boat bearing that name, which had formerly been the *Mark Lane*. She in turn was replaced in 1907 by the *Reserve No 1* boat, which was, in fact, the old *Margaret*. In 1909 the *Eleanor Brown* was fetched from the Thames boatyard where she had been built. She was the last new lifeboat to be sent to the Winterton Station.

All the beachmen were capable of taking the tiller, but the RNLI insisted on permanent coxswains for their lifeboats. William Squit Hodds filled that position from 1875 until 1898, whereupon the second coxswain, Jimmy Waite, took over until 1906. He was followed by Jimmy Moll who, in 1910, was succeeded by Sam Brown. Walter Taysh Dyble took over in 1919 and was the last Winterton lifeboat coxswain.

To be successful the beach company had to be well organised and the members had to work as a team to rules developed through experience. Each member had a share in the company and when these became available the person wishing to become a member had to be voted in as suitable. This was done by placing stones in a container, white for yes and black for no, with a majority of whites securing election. Many shares were inherited, but those that were not were sold, with the price obtained varying according to expectations. In 1900 a share made £16.5s.0d, in 1904 and 1906 shares sold for £27, and in 1908 one was bought for £32.0s.0d, but in 1912 a share only made £14 for, by then, it could be seen that the company's days were numbered.

The other financial matter of great interest to the membership was the doling out of the income. When this was to take place a flag would be hoisted on the lookout and the members would assemble to be paid. When Starchy Jnr. was voted in he was immediately given the job of dividing

48. The Beachmen who broke up the hulk of the barque *Chili,* 1902. George Beck is on the right.

49. The lifeboat *Eleanor Brown* on the 7th September 1909, the day she officially joined the No.2 Station. From left to right; on the beach, George Larner, Sam Brown, Ben Popay, George 'Plug' Smith, and Fred George. In the boat; Jimmy Moll, George Beck, Tom Thirtle, John George, Henry Smith, George King, Albert George, Henry Goffin, Joseph Larner, Robert Brown, Joe Haylett, Billy Powles, John Smith, Harry Hovell, Walter Dyble, George Brown, Charles King, Walter Kettle, and Bob Powles.

up the spoils for, as he put it, 'the old men used to make a fist of it'. The reason he was given the job was that he had been a schoolteacher for a year and thus was considered to be an educated man. The old men used to implore him to 'dole it up close', i.e. make sure every last halfpenny was shared out. One share was always retained for the upkeep of the boats, gear and shed, and two shares were paid to the RNLI, if the lifeboat had been launched. To be entitled to a dole, a member had to have actually been involved in the salvage job in question.

Vigilance was essential if the Winterton boat was to be the first to arrive at a casualty. During the day there were plenty of beachmen around to man the lookout, but at night a special watch had to be organised. Between 10.00 pm and 7.00 am three men would take it in turns to scan the sea from the lookout. Lots were drawn at Christmas for these watches. Skippers and others with business interests could pay to have theirs done for them. Starchy Jnr. paid his father-in-law, Charlie Scuddy King, 2s.0d a night for this service.

The beach company shed was lined with lockers in which were kept dry clothes and boots. When the beachmen were on night watch they took it in turns to sleep on these lockers. In the seaward facing walls were a number of shuttered square holes through which telescopes could be thrust. One of these telescopes was presented to the beachmen by the Wilson Line for services rendered to the *SS. Martello* in 1902.

Although the amalgamation of the two companies ended the rivalry at sea it did nothing to stop the deep division that existed between those who fished from north of the gap and those who did so from the south. It is unclear how the old rivals managed to work together in the new company, but what is evident is that the two groups of fishermen exhibited entirely different characteristics, with one serving God and the other Mammon.

At one end of the North Shed was a pulpit, on which lay a large bible. Services were regularly held there on Sundays, when one of the beachmen preachers, such as Dennis Leech, would officiate. Most of the North Shed men would not go to sea on a Saturday night nor on a Sunday. When a ship came ashore one Sunday in the late 19th Century, Wilks Larner launched a boat, but could not get the chapel men to join him.

By contrast the South Shed, which was rebuilt in 1906, was known as the 'Devil's Den' or 'Tramps Den'. In there, men smoked, swore, brawled, and gambled, if, that is, they could see each other through the pall of blue smoke that filled the room. Girls were forbidden to go anywhere near the South Shed, whereas the fisher boys were enticed in, so they could be relieved of their fishing money by the card playing older men. This rivalry lasted beyond the First World War.

Up until the 1860s Winterton men made a living from 'longshoring, salvaging, and deep-sea fishing, the latter confined to the Spring mackerel and the Autumn herring fisheries. These fisheries amounted to three to four months work a year, scarcely enough to make boat owning an attractive proposition, especially as mortgages had to be taken out to purchase them. This all changed with the introduction of trawling.

Trawling from Yarmouth started on a small scale in the 1840s and remained relatively unimportant until 1855-6, when a large number of smacks moved from Barking to the port, most notably Samuel Hewett's Short Blue Fleet. The reason for the move was to reduce costs by being closer to the fishing grounds.

The advantage of trawling was that it could be pursued all the year round and by 1875 there were 400 trawling smacks working from Yarmouth and Gorleston. It was usual for these smacks to make a six-week voyage, the vessels sailing in fleets under the control of an experienced skipper,

50. Beachmen in front of the company shed and lookout, c1905. From left to right; Lew Powles, Jimmy Hodds, —, George Larner (holding a company telescope), Josiah Haylett, Charlie Bessey, Ephraim Hodds, Edgar Hodds, and Robert Hodds.

51. Group of fisherboys outside the South Shed (Devil's Den), c1910. From left to right; seated, Charles Sheals and Harold Brown. Standing, George King, Walter Kettle, Jack Haylett, Rolly Hovell, Percy King, Stanley Hewitt, Lenny Brown, Walter Brown, Alfred Hodds, Charlie Moll, Ted Hodds, Ted Sheals, and —- Hovell.

who was known as the 'Admiral of the Fleet'. Each fleet had in attendance fast sailing cutters to take the catch to the London market. But there were also 'single boaters', i.e. boats that made weekly trips and short voyages. Some of these worked with the fleets, others landed their catches at Yarmouth to be sent by rail to London.

The concept of single boating appealed to the Winterton men, but they worked herring luggers, which were significantly different from trawling smacks. The lugger was of slighter build and carried lugsails, for it was only necessary to sail to the fishing grounds, cast the nets, and drift with the tide. The latter were heavier and sported a smack or dandy rig suitable for towing a trawl. The answer was the introduction of what were called 'converter' smacks, i.e. boats which could be rigged for both types of fishing. In the late 1860s this innovation, together with the prospect of all the year round fishing, tempted several Winterton men into boat owning.

First to do so was a partnership comprising two brothers, Walter and Henry George, together with Henry's brother-in-law, Dennis Leech, and Charles Powles. In 1868 they bought a new boat, which they named the *Band of Hope*, after the beach company yawl of that name. To finance her purchase they borrowed £270 from the Mack brothers, the boat's builders, £100 from Capt. George King, the promoter of the Goole migration, and £40 from Dennis's father, Edward Leech.

In 1871 they bought an old boat, the *Kestrel*, which was immediately mortgaged to fish salesman John Malden, to secure £100. In 1877, however, the partnership was dissolved when Walter George decided to leave. Dennis Leech and Henry George took the *Band of Hope*, whilst Charles Powles and his son James took the *Kestrel*, which for some reason was broken up the following year.

In early 1871 two more boats were registered to Winterton owners, the *Alarm* and the *Two*

Brothers. The *Alarm*, built in 1847, was bought by George Diboll from William Utting, who lent him £100 to enable him to do so. The *Two Brothers* was a different proposition. She was built in 1866 and bought from John Nelson by Robert Brown and his brother Maurice. Both had been fishermen but, at the time of purchase, were carpenters. She too was mortgaged to John Malden, to secure £300. In 1875 Robert died and Maurice became the sole owner.

The 1871 census provides a snapshot of these boats at work for, on census night, the 2nd April, they were out trawling. Although mostly registered as luggers, they were dandy rigged for that purpose. The *Band of Hope* was in the North Sea, skippered by Henry George, with a Winterton crew, including his brother, Isaiah, as mate. The *Kestrel* was 'lying to at sea W.N.W. of Yarmouth, 100 miles' skippered by Dennis Leech. His crew was largely made up of Winterton men. The *Alarm* was also in the North Sea, skippered by Robert Warnes with a Winterton crew. Finally the *Two Brothers* was in the care of James Gilbert George. His Winterton crew included John Toll Goffin as mate, Edward George, and a young Wilks Larner. Another 25 boats out trawling had Winterton born crewmen.

Later that year brothers Edward and Dennis Punch George, together with Robert Goffin and Joseph Haylett, formed a partnership to buy a new boat from the Mack brothers, which they named the *Adviser*. The mortgage they took out on her to secure £294 was discharged in 1876. In January 1875 Goffin and Haylett sold their share in the boat to the George brothers, who shortly afterwards bought the *Holmesdale*, which they promptly mortgaged to the Mack brothers to secure £250. Both boats were registered as dandy rigged.

Goffin and Haylett then bought an old lugger called the *Charlotte*. She had been built in 1843 and in March 1877 they sold her to Walter George. By then they had already acquired the newly

52. Dennis Olley Leech, c1865. Fishing boat owner and lay preacher.

53. Walter George, c1895. Fishing boat owner and lay preacher.

built *Heartsease*, which they mortgaged to fish salesman J.W. de Caux. Like many Winterton boats she was built by the Mack brothers and was dandy rigged. Finally in 1872 James Amis and his brother-in-law, Robert George, bought the lugger *Olive Branch*.

This fishing revolution was seen as significant enough by the local correspondent of the Yarmouth Independent to warrant comment. On the 30th January 1875 he wrote, under the heading Winterton; 'One of our large trawlers Adviser the property of Messes. George of this place, has again commenced trawling, and we understand, has sailed to join the fleet. What a difference now to what it was a few years ago when our fishermen used to commence the mackerel voyage in May and finish about the middle of July, and commence the herring voyage in the latter part of September or beginning of October, finishing about from the 10th to the 15th of December, and not going fishing again till the mackerel voyage. Now almost as soon as the finish of the herring voyage they commence trawling, and continue so until herring voyage again, and it will be seen that our fishermen are at home but very little. We also understand that the other large boats will shortly commence the trawling among them the Charlotte, lately purchased by Messrs. R. Goffin and J. Haylett; and we wish them all success'.[49]

Seven years later, in 1882, John Starchy George and Robert Roland George, sons of Edward and Dennis, bought a new boat from the Mack brothers, which they named the *Robert and John*. She was dandy rigged and as usual was mortgaged to her builders.

Most of these new boat owners were successful skippers who wanted a greater share in the money earned by their skill and endeavour. They reasoned that all the year round fishing would pay off the mortgage on these boats, with a tidy sum left over. But skill was not enough to secure success in the fishing business, for that rare commodity depended on so many factors.

As far as the herring and mackerel fisheries were concerned, supply and demand had to be in

54. The Market Place, c1900. The general shop was kept by Frederick Isaiah George.

55. Robert Goffin and family posing in their Sunday best, c1895. Robert was in partnership with Joseph Haylett as boat owners in the age of sail. Left to right; sitting on the floor, Bessie and Robert. Sitting and standing, Anna, Robert, Elsie, Annis, Selina, and Julia.

balance if a steady income was to be made. A glut would ruin the price and too few fish would mean high prices, but a lower overall take. The quality of the fish was also important and bad weather was a mixed blessing, for while it would limit the number of boats that went out, it could also damage the gear or cause it to be lost altogether, which would prove very costly. Fluctuations in demand would also affect the final outcome.

In the early 1870s the returns from these fisheries were reasonable enough, encouraging men to become involved, but later in the decade and throughout the black 1880s there were many poor seasons, with boat owners scarcely covering their costs, let alone being able to pay off their mortgages and take money home.

At the same time the Yarmouth trawl fishery went into terminal decline as the grounds within easy reach became fished out, the railway companies favoured Lowestoft, and a major competitor, Grimsby, went over to steam trawlers.

These events resulted in a disastrous period for the Winterton boat owners as one by one they went out of business. In 1872 George Diboll's *Alarm* was sold from under him as he had defaulted on his mortgage, and in similar circumstances Amis and George lost the *Olive Branch*, although it has to be said that these failures may have as much to do with the competency of the men concerned than the state of the fisheries.

In 1878 the *Kestrel* was broken up and in 1880 the Mack brothers sold the *Band of Hope* for mortgage non-repayment. In 1884 the *Two Brothers* was also broken up and her registry closed.

Edward and Dennis George continued to fish until 1889, but by then they could see no hope of clearing their debts so they declared themselves bankrupt. At the Hearing Edward stated that; 'No creditor had taken proceedings against them, but they stopped because they had no money to go on with… The boats this season earned £459 each, and that did not more than pay expenses'.[50] The mortgagees, J. W. De Caux, and the Mack brothers, promptly sold the *Adviser* and the *Holmesdale*.

Starchy and Roland fared no better for in 1890 the Mack brothers took their boat the *Robert and John*. This caused ill feeling in the George family with Robert's mother blaming John for the failure. Finally, in 1892, Goffin and Haylett sold the *Heartsease* to Horatio Fenner, and that was the end of that.

As for the men themselves, several continued to skipper for Yarmouth owners, but others such as Dennis George, Henry George, and Robert Goffin gave up deep sea fishing and became shopkeepers in the village.

There was, however, one Winterton man who bucked the trend and that was Wilks Larner, the 'Fisher King of Yarmouth', a veritable legend in his own lifetime. Wilks was born in 1851 and, as with most Winterton boys, when the time came he took a berth as a boy cook on a sailing lugger. As has already been mentioned, he sailed with Winterton skipper, James Gilbert George, and it was from him that he learned his trade.

By the late 1870s Wilks had become a skipper and had formed a working partnership with Yarmouth smack owner William Crome. This proved very profitable for both parties. Crome owned a number of smacks and Wilks skippered them all, none more successfully than the *Clupidae* and the *Concordia*.

The home fishing of 1884 was the start of an unparalleled run of seven years when each season Wilks topped the Yarmouth earnings list, a remarkable feat considering the unpredictable nature of the work. Successful skippers were called 'lucky', but Wilks must have possessed much more than luck to be so consistent throughout the dark days of the herring fishery.

In 1891, however, this remarkable run came to an abrupt end for reasons given in the Yarmouth Independent of 24th October. Under the headline 'Accident to "Josh" Wilkes', the paper reported

56. The village viewed from the sea-bank, c1920.

57. James 'Gilbert' George, c1870.

58. William 'Wilks' Larner, c1885. The 'Fisher King of Yarmouth'.

that; 'The Clupidae, owned by Mr. Crome, of Yarmouth, landed at Caister on Saturday her skipper, so well known in Yarmouth as "Josh" Wilkes, who had been seriously injured at sea. On Tuesday her nets became foul with a Frenchman's, and while heaving in his warp the unfortunate man was crushed in the capstan. Wilkes, for 7 years, has placed his season's catch at the head of the list of Yarmouth boats, and the trade generally will regret to learn that he now lies in a precarious condition'.[51]

He was soon on the mend for the following week the same newspaper was able to report; 'We are pleased to hear Mr. William Larner, our local "fishing king", is recovering from his accident. It is hoped he will be well in time to keep up his fishing voyage to the highest record'.[52]

But Wilks had other plans. Getting back on his feet he bought a sailing trawler, the *Gorleston*, and with him at the helm she quickly earned a reputation as a 'lucky' boat in both single boating and fleeting with the Short Blue Fleet. Things went well for over five years then fate once more intervened. In 1897 Wilks decided to visit his daughter in Manchester, allowing his brother-in-law, Walter Spot Kettle, to skipper the boat while he was away. This proved to be a costly mistake for off the Dutch coast the trawler caught fire and, after blazing for some hours, sank.

One wonders what Wilks said to his brother-in-law on his return, but at 45 he had had enough of deep-sea fishing and 'retired' to the beach. It is said that the lads at the time would look at Wilks in the same way a young able seaman would look at an admiral.

With Wilks working from Yarmouth there was no Winterton based deep sea fishing industry throughout most of the 1890s, although the fishermen continued to crew for Yarmouth owners. Then came the steam drifter and with it a whole new chapter in Winterton boat owning, but to understand how this came about it is necessary to go back to the time of the migration.

When the Winterton men took up boat owning in the late 1860s their relatives, who had settled in Caister and Yarmouth, did likewise, with most of them sharing the same fate in the dark days.

At Caister, however, three migrant family concerns managed to keep going, those of Robert Leech Plummer and his son John, Walter Haylett and his son Edwin, and Old Jimmy Haylett's son George. At Yarmouth, Jacob George, and his son Jack, also survived into the age of steam.

Jacob and his brother Philip George had migrated to Caister in the 1850s, both marrying local girls. Philip served with distinction as coxswain of the lifeboat, between 1872 and 1887, and remained there for the rest of his life. Around 1868 Jacob moved to Yarmouth and, after his death in 1893, his widow and their son Jack ran the fishing business he had started. Jacob and Philip were brothers of the Edward and Dennis, who had owned the *Adviser* and the *Holmesdale*.

Returning to Winterton, after losing the *Robert and John*, Starchy skippered boats for various owners including his cousin Jack. This proved to be his way back into boat owning. Reporting on the herring fishery of 1898, G. H. Harris wrote; 'The year 1898 may be taken, too, as signalising the advent of the steam drifter, which must be carefully distinguished, of course, from the steam trawler. Steam drifters are not a novelty, but their muster has been too small to exercise an appreciable influence in the trade. This year they numbered twenty, and can no longer be reckoned a negligible quantity. Probably they are destined to extirpate the sailing lugger…'. He went on to say that; 'It would not pay to build a steamer that could follow her business for three months only and lay up on the 'hard' for the rest of the year, as the old luggers did. But if a plan can be found whereby she can drift for the better part of the year, she may pay. And apparently, in the development of the West Coast and Irish fishings, such a place has been found'.[53]

The following year was reckoned, at the time, to be the best ever. Exported barrels of fish increased from 45,872 to 141,585, chiefly to Russia and Germany. It was the start of an

59. The sailing trawler *Gorleston* YH840, 1893. Painted by A Dobson. She was owned by 'Wilks' Larner until destroyed by fire in 1897.

60. John 'Starchy' George and family, c1900. John is wearing the type of collar that earned him his nickname. The three boys all became drifter owners. Left to right; John Jnr., John, Julia Jnr., Basil, Ellen, Julia, and Horace.

unprecedented period of success for the herring industry, with improvement year on year culminating in the spectacular season of 1913.

In 1899 the steam drifter *Lottie* was built for Jimmy Pitchers Jnr., a man who had a close association with Winterton and its people. Starchy skippered her from new and when a year later she was sold to his cousin, Jack George, he stayed with her. In 1900 he bought a quarter share in the boat and in 1903 acquired the remainder. She was the first Winterton owned steam drifter.

In 1906 Jack George bought a new boat, which he named the *Boy Jacob*, after one of his sons. After netting and running her for the home fishing he sold her to Starchy. It was in her that in 1909 Starchy Jnr. first went to sea as a skipper.

Going from strength to strength, Starchy bought another drifter, naming her the *Boy Eddie* after his youngest son. His second son, Horace Social, promptly took her to sea, to avoid being examined for a skipper's ticket, a requirement that was to come in that year. In 1912 Jack George bought a new drifter, the *Ocean Spray*, netted and fished her for six weeks, before selling her on to his cousin. Finally in 1914, Starchy ordered the first drifter to be built in Colby's yard at Lowestoft, a boat he called the *Ellen and Irene* after his two youngest daughters. By then his sons, Starchy Jnr. and Social were in partnership with him.

Not far behind Starchy was Frederick Kyfer Goffin, and a partnership of Jack Punch George and Dennis Flinny Goffin. In 1903 Jimmy Pitchers Jnr. bought the *Ivy* and the following year took Kyfer in with him as an equal partner. Norford Suffling, the fish salesman, acquired Pitchers' share in 1905 and three years later Kyfer became her sole owner. In 1910 he bought the newly built *Girl Nancy*, naming her after one of his daughters.

In 1903 Jack George bought the *Gertrude*, fished her for a season then sold her to Punch and Flinny. Unfortunately she was lost in 1910, near the Haisborough lightship, but shortly before this they had bought the *W Elliott*. In 1911 they acquired the *Fern*, which, having been built in 1902, was quite old by the rapidly improving standards of the day.

Walter Toody Rudd was another of the owners helped into business by Jack George. In 1907 they jointly purchased the *Silver Spray*, with Toody borrowing his share of the cost from his partner. In 1911 he bought the *Dashing Spray*, which he took to sea while his brother, Robert, skippered the *Silver Spray*.

In 1908 two more Winterton skippers took to boat owning, Dennis Cuddy George, and Jack Waite. Cuddy had first gone to sea at the age of 10, with his uncle Dennis. With finance from Elliott and Garrood, he bought the *Young Archie*, named after his son, and in 1914 acquired the *Norford Suffling*.

Jack Waite was the nephew of Jimmy Waite, who kept the Fisherman's Return. It was Jimmy who provided the capital for this venture. In 1908 Jack bought the *Lerwick* in partnership with John Mair of Peterhead, and in 1912 he bought the *Sweet Pea*.

In 1909 Robert Roland George, the ex-partner of Starchy in the failed *Robert and John* enterprise, ventured back into boat owning with the *Harry*. In 1913 George Jilts Woodhouse bought the *Charm* from Jack George, thereby starting his own fishing business. In 1917 he took in as a partner his brother Henry.

In 1902 Commander James Bloomfield arrived in Yarmouth to work for the Smith's Dock Trust Company Ltd., and quickly formed a friendship with Winterton skipper William James Empson Green, known as Wee because of his great size. In 1907 they joined forces to buy the newly built

61. The *Lottie* YH434, c1905. Built in 1899 she was the first steam drifter to be owned in Winterton. Left to right; John George, (skipper/owner), —, Horace George, —, Sam Larner, —, —, —, and Sid Cator.

62. The *Ellen and Irene* YH272, 1914. Built for John George she was the first steam drifter to be launched from Colby's Yard at Lowestoft. John is seen with his daughter Ellen about to perform the launching ceremony.

Ocean Gift. In 1911 Bloomfield formed his own company, Bloomfields Ltd, and took over Wee's share in the boat.

In 1914 Wee set up W. J. E. Green Ltd, and bought the *Ocean Reaper* from Bloomfields. He had not long returned from a twelve-week voyage in the White Sea to prospect for herring in the aptly named *Ocean Comrade*. He failed to find new fishing grounds, but made valuable contacts and taught the Russians drift net fishing.

Bloomfield had the knack of employing the best skippers and he retained their services by taking them in as co-partners. In 1914 the *Ocean Guide* was launched from Chambers yard at Lowestoft, with Bloomfields owning 2/3rds and Walter Scuddy King the other 1/3rd. Later in the year the same arrangement was made with his brother Bob Scuddy in respect of the *Ocean Trust*.

With the population of the village remaining much the same until the first decade of the 20th Century, there was no real increase in the number of houses until that time. There was, however, the gradual process of demolition of the old thatched cottages and the building of brick and tile replacements, with the sons and grandsons of Samuel Larner doing much of the work. Around 1892 they built a large eight-roomed house at the back of The Clink for Wilks Larner, which he called Albion House. Unfortunately this was damaged in the Second World War and subsequently demolished.

In 1876 a new Primitive Methodist Chapel was built in the Market Place to replace the small one in The Clink. The following year a room for infants was added to the school at a cost of £600, but the restoration of the medieval parish church was the most significant change to take place at this time. In 1859 the west window and two of the south windows were reconstructed and a stone reredos was installed, but the major works were carried out in 1877 and 1878, at the behest of Mrs. Hume of Hill House, the daughter of the Rev. John Nelson. She funded the restoration in commemoration of her late husband, William Burnley Hume, who died in 1876. The work was designed by architect Herbert J. Green and built by William Hubbard of East Dereham. The alterations included a new roof, built to the profile of the former medieval one, the rebuilding of the upper nave and chancel walls, to which were added crenellated parapets, and the reconstruction of most of the windows. There were also many internal alterations. The result is a splendid fusion of medieval and Gothic Revival architecture.

The most specialist buildings to be erected during this period were the warehouses of the deep-sea fishing boat owners. Some of these owners lived in the village but ran their boats from Yarmouth. Others built warehouses in Winterton where they stored and maintained their gear, especially their nets.

There may have been warehouses in the early days of sail but, if there were, they can no longer be identified, or have been demolished. Three are known from the sailing era of this period, those of Dennis Leech, Edward George, and Goffin and Haylett, all built in The Clink.

With the advent of the steam drifter came a new wave of construction. Between 1905 and 1910 warehouses were built in Low Road for Punch and Flinny, Starchy, and Kyfer. Toody and Cuddy built theirs in Bulmer Lane and Jack Waite had one on the west side of North Market Road.

In the early part of the 20th Century two new housing areas were developed in the village, one in The Clink and the other along Bulmer Lane. In 1900 Jimmy Pitchers bought a large piece of land between North Market Road and the dunes from Henry George. This was known as the Twine Ground. On the 19th March that year his builder, H. Futter, started the construction of seven houses, designed by architect C. Baker. Over the next year or so he completed 24 houses in three terraces, which he called Miriam Terrace, May Cottages, and Snowdrop Cottages, the latter being dated the

63. The Market Place, c1910. The Primitive Methodist Chapel was built in 1875 and the general shop had recently been acquired by William Sims.

64. Family members and workers of Jack 'Punch' George and Dennis 'Flinny' Goffin, 1905. They are seen posing beside their newly built warehouse. In the background is the warehouse of 'Kyfer' Goffin, fronting Low Road. Between the two buildings stands Kyfer's tanning copper. Left to right; front row, Walter George, May George, Eliza Hodds, Myrtle Hodds, Betsey Goffin, Anna Goffin, Jack George. Back row; Jack George, Henry Goffin, Polly Hewitt, Thirza George, Selina Goffin, Libby Hodds, Fred Goffin, and Dennis Goffin.

7th June 1901. Numbers 1–5 Miriam Terrace were bought by Starchy to house his five children, with him taking up residence in nearby Beaconsfield House.

In 1904 the same builder bought a piece of land in Bulmer Lane, against the pond (the Bull Mere) and constructed two villas. Over the next decade the frontage on the west side was gradually built up, with several of the houses being occupied by the newly successful steam drifter owners. This earned for Bulmer Lane the nickname 'Gold Street'. In 1905, on the other side, Jimmy Waite started the construction of a boarding house, which was opened in July 1906. It was later called The Mariners, taking the licence from The Three Mariners on the latter's closure in 1955, but it has since been demolished.

Further south, Bulmer Lane becomes the Hemsby Road and here, until 1902, stood a large post mill, run by the Starling family. There had probably been a mill on the site for centuries and this one bore the date 1700. On the 6th April that year, a freak gale from the north-east, struck the village and before Austic Starling, the miller, could release the sails, the entire top structure came crashing down, shattering the carcass of the mill in the process. It was a sad end to a well-known local landmark.

Nall's comment about nicknames being rife in Winterton has already been noted. With so many people in one place with the same forename and surname, it was necessary to come up with a way of distinguishing them one from another. The answer was for everyone to have a unique nickname. Once given to an individual, however, the nickname would be passed down, and more often than not would, for all practical purposes, replace the surname. Charles King was nicknamed Scuddy

65. Bulmer Lane, looking north, c1920. The houses on the left were built between 1904 and 1911. Several were owned by successful drifter owners, earning the Lane the nickname 'Gold Street'.

and his sons were known as Bob Scuddy, Arthur Scuddy, Walter Scuddy, Charlie Scuddy, Ted Scuddy, and Jack Scuddy.

These nicknames survive in oral tradition from the mid 19th Century, but their meanings have usually been lost. This is not surprising when one considers how a nickname like Starchy was coined. John George, who was first given the nickname, had a brother, Robert Lugar George. Robert went 'big boating' and lived for a time in London. When John used to visit him he would put on a starched collar, a rare sight in the village, hence the nickname. Cuddy on the other hand was simply the surname of a man Dennis George went round with as a boy.

5. 1914-1939

The home fishing of 1913 turned out to be the best ever. In simple terms 825,000,000 herrings were caught by 999 drifters, grossing £1,000,000. Fishermen, owners, buyers and curers all had a good season and the boats were packed so tightly in the harbour that it was possible to walk across them from bank to bank. Then came the First World War and the herring fishing was never the same again.

The war officially started on the 4th August 1914, but long before then its inevitability was obvious and preparations had already been made to augment the Navy. On the 28th July the coastguards were called up and in early August the men of the Royal Naval Reserve (RNR) were told to report. This organisation was established in 1859 to recruit men from amongst the merchant marine and fishermen, who could be called up in the event of war. At the outset each recruit received a month's paid training and a retainer thereafter.

Attracted by the pay and the uniform, many Winterton fishermen enrolled and were subsequently called up, some entering the regular Navy, but most joining what would later be termed the Patrol Service. There was also another reservist organisation, the Royal Naval Volunteer Reserve (RNVR), and some Winterton men entered the senior service via this route.

The Patrol Service was something of a navy within a navy as it consisted of requisitioned trawlers and drifters, crewed largely by the fishermen of the RNR. As far as trawlers were concerned, they tended to be taken with their crews and deployed on decoy duties, minesweeping, and submarine hunting. The drifters did not have such a close relationship with their own skippers and crews and were mostly used for harbour work. The pick of the Yarmouth drifter fleet was employed in this way, leaving only the older steam drifters to continue to fish throughout the war, largely for home consumption, as the overseas markets were no longer accessible.

66. The steam drifter *Silver Spray* YH175, c1910. Owned by Walter 'Toody' Rudd.

67. William 'Wee' Green and wife Rosa, taken on their wedding day.

68. Walter 'Scuddy' King and family, c1915. Walter is wearing his Skipper's RN uniform.

Nearly all the Winterton boats were requisitioned, their owners receiving monthly payments from the Government, and the RNR Winterton fishermen were posted to vessels around the British Isles and further afield. Those with skipper's tickets were given the rank of Skipper R.N. and placed in charge of the requisitioned fishing boats.

Starchy Jnr. was given command of the *Ocean Warrior*, working at Belfast, in the Examination Service. Each harbour had two such boats, on board one of which was a naval lieutenant, who would be ferried out to new arrivals to check their papers. If the papers were in order the vessel was given the appropriate signal flags and allowed to proceed to the docks.

Three Winterton owned, or part owned, *Ocean* boats were requisitioned in September 1914. The *Ocean Guide* was fitted with a three-pounder naval gun and sent on patrol, the *Ocean Reward* received a six-pounder anti-aircraft gun and served as a water tender at naval bases, as did the *Ocean Reaper*. The *Ocean Trust* was not requisitioned until November 1918, when the Admiralty chartered her for £39.3s.11d a month.

To the fishermen, being able to wear a naval uniform made them feel special and they could not wait to visit a photographer in their designated port to have the fact recorded for their relatives back home. Many such photographs are to be found in local collections, taken in such places as Londonderry, Sheerness, Dover, Liverpool, Belfast, and Larne.

Of all the men who served at this time, one merits special attention and that is Wee Green. Being in the RNR Wee was called up on the 10th August 1914 and, before being demobbed on the 21st December 1918, achieved the rank of Chief Skipper. It was during the early part of this service that he was accredited with having invented the anti-submarine net, to protect the entrances to harbours. Shortly after the war Walter Wood wrote; 'It is claimed, and perhaps time will show that the claim is not unjustly made, that the employment of nets in connection with the trapping of the earliest of the German submarines originated with an East Coast drifter skipper. Let the claim be considered, and it will be obvious that at the least the submarine catching at the outset was a development of the system of catching herrings with the drift-nets'.[54]

That the man in question was Wee Green was confirmed by his son Eddie who recalled that; 'Father was in the *Ocean Reaper* during the First World War. He had the idea of using the herring net to stop submarines in the same way it catches herring. He suggested this to the Admiralty who took it up and developed it using steel for the net. He didn't get any payment because he was in the Navy'. There was no real official recognition of his contribution to the war effort, although his service record does carry the observation 'showing zeal & ability, being of great assistance in respect of net-laying'.[55]

Only two Winterton boats succumbed to the rigours of the war, the *Boy Eddie*, which was eaten by beetle at Brindisi, and the *W Elliott*. In 1918 the *W Elliott*, skippered by J Mair, was part of a force hunting a submarine in the Straits of Dover, which was attacked by German warships. Eight boats were sunk, including the *W Elliott*.

But loss of property is nothing compared to loss of life and the churchyard war-memorial records the names of 18 men who died in the First World War. The majority were RNR seamen but, as a reminder of the fact that not all Winterton men went to sea, six had been in the Army, five of whom, from the 7th Battalion of the Norfolk Regiment, were killed-in-action on the Western Front.

With the war ending in November 1918, the Admiralty no longer needed the requisitioned drifters and over the next two years the surviving Winterton boats were returned. Four years of war had taken its toll on the herring fishery and the seas were still mined. The pre-war boat owners

69. The steam drifter *W Elliott* YH 423, c1910. Owned before the First World War by Jack 'Punch' George and Dennis 'Flinny' Goffin. She was sunk by enemy action in February 1918. Left to right; Charlie Leech, Jack George, —, —, —, Fred Lown, Highty Gallant, and —.

70. The 'Starchy' George family warehouse in Low Road, c1910. Left to right; Horace George, John George (owner), Basil George, John George Jnr., and Harry Moll (ransacker).

had to decide whether a resumption of fishing was worthwhile. Given that they had made good money in the decade before the war and had also been well paid for the use of their boats during the war, it is surprising that so few decided to retire. Most sent their boats to sea again, but of course fishing was in their blood.

Those who finished were Starchy, Cuddy, Toody, and Jack Waite, who moved away from the village. Those who resumed were Starchy Jnr. and his brother Social with the *Ocean Spray*, Punch and Flinny with the *Fern*, Kyfer with the *Girl Nancy*, Jilts and Henry Woodhouse with the *Charm*, and Wee Green with the *Ocean Reaper*, the *WPG*, and the *Ocean Roamer*. Two men still had part ownership in Bloomfield boats, Walter Scuddy with the *Ocean Guide* and Elijah John Green with the *Ocean Reward*, although he sold his share back to Bloomfields in 1921. Most of these boats had been built before 1914, but the *WPG*, the *Ocean Roamer*, and the *Ocean Lover* (formerly HMD *Gale*) had been built during the war or shortly thereafter. Wee Green had bought them even though he was a serving Skipper, the *WPG* being named after his parents William and Phyllis Green.

No doubt these boat owners and the returning Winterton fishermen hoped for a resumption of the good years, but the war had all but destroyed the most important requirement of a successful herring fishery and that was demand for the fish. In 1928 the editor of the Transactions of the Norfolk and Norwich Naturalists Society wrote; 'The success of the Yarmouth herring fishery depends, in the last analysis, upon the capacity of the European peasant to consume salted herrings during the winter. It is not a question of organising a fleet and equipping it to catch herrings, but entirely a matter of marketing the catch, for 95 per cent of the fish landed has to find a foreign destination'.[56]

The main pre-war markets had been Germany, which was now too impoverished to buy the fish and Russia, which being in the throes of revolution was largely inaccessible. Add to this foreign competition and the usual variables of damaged gear, gluts and poor quality fish, then it can be readily appreciated that the 1920s was not a good time to be herring fishing.

Circumstances did improve, however, as markets became re-established and this encouraged the ever-optimistic boat owners to expand their businesses and more skippers to venture into boat owning. Only the 1921, 1925, and 1928 seasons were really bad and although the fleet was steadily ageing, new drifters were still being built.

Having bought the *Ocean Spray* from their father Starchy Jnr. took her to sea, while his brother, Social, skippered the *Jack George* until they were able to buy the *Thirty-Two* from the Smith's Dock Trust Company Ltd. In 1923 they bought the *Rose and Gladys*, which had been owned by a man called Tom Moore. She had been skippered by Charlie Leech, of Winterton who, when asked by a Lowestoft man what the TM on the funnel stood for, replied 'Tons of Money'. Shortly afterwards Moore went bankrupt. In 1925 they bought the *Golden Gain* and sold the *Thirty-Two*.

Managing these boats required the brothers to spend time ashore, but Social always wanted to be at sea. He was one of the top skippers, a man who would go out in all weathers, his philosophy being 'You can't earn a living in the harbour'. His brother, however, thought he took too many chances with the gear. As a result, in 1928, they decided to go their separate ways, Starchy Jnr. taking the *Rose and Gladys* and the *Golden Gain* and Social the *Ocean Spray*.

In 1920 the Woodhouse brothers bought the *Twenty-Eight*, a boat, which had the wooden framing and roof of her wheelhouse blown off during a gale off Yarmouth. In 1926 they acquired the *Dusty Miller* from George Tuck and in 1928 sold the *Twenty-Eight* to John Finlay of Banff, having already bought the *Queen of the Fleet*. In 1931 they bought the *Achievable*.

In 1919 Wee added the *Ocean Lover* to the three boats he already owned, and in 1924 bought the *Ocean Swell*. In July 1925 he decided to run them himself, for until then they had been managed

71. The steam drifter *Ocean Spray* YH264, Yarmouth harbour, c1933. She was owned and skippered by Horace 'Social' George. The crew are cleaning the nets on the Gorleston side prior to moving over to Yarmouth to sell the catch.

72. Tanning the nets, c1905. The tanning copper belonged to Jack Waite and stood near his warehouse on North Market Road. Left to right; on the copper, Jack Waite and Dennis 'Cuddy' George; others, Henry Smith, 'Wilks' Larner, and Robert Hodds.

by Bloomfields. Perhaps the death of his friend, Commander Bloomfield, in 1922 had something to do with this decision. In 1929 he bought the *Pimpernel* and renamed her the *Phyllis Rose* before, in 1930, selling her to Alfred and Charles Powles. The same year the *Rose Hilda* joined his fleet. She was the last brand new boat to be bought by a Winterton owner.

Before the war Walter Scuddy had owned the *Ocean Guide*, in partnership with Bloomfields. In 1919 he formed his own company, Walter J. King Ltd., taking over Bloomfield's share in the boat in the process. In 1925 he sold her back to Bloomfields, having bought the *Ascendent* the previous year.

In 1922 Toody came out of retirement and bought the *Rambling Rose*, and in 1924 the *Romany Rose*. Cuddy resumed fishing in 1925 with the newly built *Plankton*. In 1930 he sold her and bought the *Supporter*. At the same time he became the ship's husband, or manager, for Norford Suffling Ltd.

Shortly after Cuddy returned to the fishing three other owners decided to retire. Punch and Flinny ran the *Fern* until selling her to Charles Bullard in 1927, and the following year Kyfer sold the *Girl Nancy*.

The ownerships so far described originated before the First World War, but as the decade wore on so new owners began to appear. The first of these was Powley Dick Green, Wee's brother, who in 1923 bought the *Oakland*. Three years later he acquired the *Manx Bride*, renaming her the *PAG* after his daughters Patsy and Audrey. Finally, in 1930, he bought the *Plankton* from Cuddy. This was the last small fleet to be assembled by a Winterton man, the other new owners running single boat affairs.

In 1926 Walter Nuts Powles and William Symonds bought the *EBC* in equal shares, but in 1928 Symonds sold his half to John Breach and she was re-registered at Lowestoft. She retained her name, but became LT364. Charlie Leech acquired the *Viking*, but soon sold her again. In 1927, a younger brother of Starchy Jnr., Basil Bill George, bought the *Erin*, which he renamed the *Aspiration*. She in turn gave way in 1929 to the much newer *Resurge*.

In 1928 Stanley Bounty Hewitt bought the *Girl Nancy* from Kyfer, but in 1930 he sold her to another new Winterton owner, John Ducky Chaney, who had the backing of the Pitchers family. Bounty then bought the *Young Ernie*, which, having been built in 1924, was a more modern boat.

In 1929 Jimmy Annison (formerly Brown) went into business with the *Sphinx*, but quickly sold her and bought the *Receptive*. That same year Jack Roker Hodds bought the *Ocean Warrior* from Bloomfields, and Robert Rudd, Toody's brother, bought the *Radiant Rose*. In 1930 brothers Alfred and Charles Powles bought the *Phyllis Rose* from Wee.

At the beginning of the 1930s there were 17 Winterton boat owners working between them 26 steam drifters, 13 of which had been built before the outbreak of the First World War, and seven since. Significantly most of the new, single boat owners had the older boats, bought with borrowed money from the fish salesmen, especially Norford Suffling. It was not a healthy position to be in to face what the 1930s had in store for them.

The 1931 home fishing was considered to be the worst in living memory. Curers the previous year had lost heavily so they set about finding ways to avoid the same thing happening again. They shortened the season and as a result the overall catch was much smaller, yet prices were no more than half those of 1930. Commentators made the point that since the war the Yarmouth herring fishery had been dogged by dwindling catches and shrinking exports. To this was added the problem of tariffs and quotas, which had recently been introduced by some European Countries.

To the superstitious Winterton fishermen the reason for such a bad season lay much closer to home; the Stone had been moved. This black glacial boulder used to stand at the junction of The Lane with Black Street, on the western side. For many years it had been the 'village parliament', where men would gather to put the world to rights, its shininess bearing testimony to the polishing effect of countless trouser seats.

73. Boat owners and beatsters outside the warehouse in Low Road formerly used by 'Kyfer' Goffin, c1933. 'Bounty' Hewitt and 'Bill' George shared the warehouse and are sitting with their respective beatsters. Left to right; Zelia Green, Daisy Dyble, Molly Hill, Polly Hewitt, 'Bounty' Hewitt, Eva Rouse, 'Bill' George, Elsie Hodds, Ellen George, and Sarah Long.

74. A group of old men near the Stone, c1930. The removal of this glacial boulder in 1931 was thought by many to have caused that year's bad fishing, prompting its return in 1932. Left to right; Sam Larner, Will Bowgin, 'Blind Harry' Powles, Jimmy Haylett, and Fred George.

Because it was so out of place in a village of beach pebbles it was thought to have mystical powers, so when in July 1931 the County Council moved it to a yard, because it was said to be obstructing the passage of motor coaches, there was much ill feeling, especially as the fishing had failed. After months of wrangling, in February 1932, it was returned, but to a spot farther up The Lane. Seemingly it had not regained its powers for the fishing remained poor.

Things did not improve until 1936 when the season was reckoned to be the best since 1930, although for the boat owners heavy gales, particularly in November, caused considerable damage to gear and the loss of two boats. Regulations were imposed to prevent a glut and these ensured that the price of herring was well maintained. Foreign demand was also better. But it was a false dawn for 1937 was not nearly so good and 1938 was really bad in terms of quality, size of catch, and price.

These were dark days for the herring industry and for Winterton it was the 1880s all over again. Those boat owners who had made money during the good times managed to weather the storm, but many of the newcomers who were heavily in debt lost everything. The fishermen too suffered badly for, being paid by results, some seasons they took no money home at all.

In 1931 Charles Chulls Sheals bought the *Triumph*, thereby becoming the last Winterton skipper to take up boat owning before the outbreak of the Second World War. The purchase of this boat marked the peak of steam drifter owning in Winterton.

The same year Toody Rudd retired again, signing over the *Romany Rose* to his sons Walter Toody Jnr. and Charles Pop. Toody Jnr. went to sea whilst Pop managed the shore work. In 1934 Nuts Powles and Ducky Chaney were both forced to give up, and the *EBC* and the *Girl Nancy* were sold. The following year Cuddy retired for the second time, selling the *Supporter* to Billy Balls, a Yarmouth owner.

The next retirement had nothing to do with the worsening conditions. On the 6th June 1934 Donald Danky Rudd, son of Robert, won £30,000 in the Irish Sweepstake, on the Derby winner Windsor Lad. It was a veritable fortune at the time. As a result, after taking her on a pleasure trip around his old fishing haunts, Robert sold the *Radiant Rose* to Norford Suffling and gave up the fishing business.

At the end of the home fishing of 1937 the Woodhouse brothers had to finish, leaving Norford Suffling to settle their affairs. The *Achievable*, *Queen of the Fleet*, and *Dusty Miller* were all taken and sold.

By the start of 1938 all the remaining boat owners were in difficulties. In 1939 Starchy Jnr. sold the *Rose and Gladys* and the *Golden Gain* to be broken up for scrap, having bought the former Woodhouse boat *Queen of the Fleet*, for his son Jack. Sadly Jack was never to go to sea in her as he was killed at Tobruk during the Second World War.

Wee let the *WPG* (which by then was called the *Sweet Bud*) be sold for scrap, but retained his other boats. Most of the other owners managed to struggle on, some of whom owed so much they were allowed to continue, for there was nothing to be gained from forcing them to finish. Toody Jnr. managed to get in a home fishing in 1939, which was good enough to clear his debts. Three owners were forced to give up, Jack Roker, Walter Scuddy, and Powley Dick. Their boats were taken away and sold to clear debts. Apparently Jack Roker was not disastrously in debt and therefore forcing him to finish brought a return for his creditors. The *Ocean Warrior* was sold for scrap. Chulls Sheals avoided this fate by placing the *Triumph* in his wife's name.

Ironically, with the outbreak of war, the Government once more needed steam drifters for the

75. Steam drifter *Queen of the Fleet* YH530, leaving Yarmouth harbour, c1935. She was owned by George and Henry Woodhouse.

76. The sea-bank, c1910. The buildings left to right are the North Shed and lookout, the South Shed (Devil's Den), 'longshoremen's sheds, and the lifeboat house.

Patrol Service and many of the near bankrupt owners were saved by the hire fees for their boats, much to the annoyance of those who had already sold their boats cheaply or been forced to finish.

But what of the men who crewed these boats? Being share fishermen, there was no unemployment pay and therefore the 1930s was a very difficult time for them. Relief work was provided, but only for those who had made nothing at all during the season. Single men were employed to break stones in the Stokesby Pit for 10s.0d per four-day week. Married men received £1.

Strangely enough the fickle North Sea, so often the villain in the Winterton Story, came to the rescue, when in February 1938 it burst through the sea-bank at Horsey and flooded the farmland beyond. The East Suffolk and Norfolk River Board had to repair the bank and readily employed the destitute fishermen to do the work. In 1938 Sidney Nimble Empson did the 'Scotch' and home fishing as skipper of the *Girl Ena* before, in December, taking a job as general foreman with the River Board. Of the 84 men then on the books 70 were ex-fishermen.

Working from the beach also declined during the inter-war years. 'Longshore fishing, so long the bedrock of the village economy, went the way of its big brother. It held its own in the 1920s and in 1931 there were 17 boats working from the beach, five of them motorboats. The newest, however, was the six-year-old *Girl Doris*. The remainder had been built before the end of the First World War, six of them in the far off 1880s. They were still owned and run by the older fishermen/beachmen, the men who had retired from deep-sea fishing. Six years later there were only 10 boats and the *Girl Doris* was still the newest.

With the beach culture such a strong feature of Winterton tradition, the beach company survived the First World War, but the beachmen now relied on the two lifeboats to carry out their lifesaving and salvage work. By then a double lifeboat shed housed the surf lifeboat *Edward Birkbeck* and the larger *Eleanor Brown*. In January 1922 the *Edward Birkbeck* was launched to the barge *Briton* of London. One man was rescued and the vessel was saved. Later that same month the beachmen were doled £4.11s.3d for this salvage service, the last to be carried out by the beach company.

In 1923 the Cromer lifeboat station received a motor lifeboat. The following year the Winterton station was closed, the two lifeboats were removed and the beach company faded away. The lookout had been taken down in 1922, and the North Shed was demolished in 1937. In the late 1930s a yawl was still to be seen rotting on the sea-bank.

The early 1920s also witnessed the closure of the lighthouse and the scaling down of the coastguard. The lighthouse was closed in 1921 for reasons explained by Neville Long. 'By the First World War, more than four hundred yards of valley and dunes separated Winterton lighthouse from the sea and the floating lights out to sea had become so numerous and efficient, and the channel into Yarmouth Roads so well buoyed, that the presence of a lighthouse at Winterton was no longer necessary'.[57] On the 25th January 1922 the lighthouse, shorn of its equipment, was sold by auction and was converted into a holiday home.

In April 1923 the coastguard service was reduced from a chief officer and seven men to one with three men and by 1929 this had been further reduced to a chief officer and one man. In August 1934 the coastguard houses were sold by auction, fetching between £160 and £205 each.

Inshore lifesaving at Winterton now depended on the Board of Trade rocket apparatus, still under the control of the coastguard, but manned by volunteers. Bob Sorny Haylett was one of the first. He recalled that there were 14 men in the crew and that they practised four times a year, being paid 2s.6d per drill. The rocket was a boxer type, transported from the shed on a horse drawn cart. Practices made use of the pole erected in 1905 to simulate a ship's mast. This still stands on the dunes at the northern end of the village. Bob manned the rocket for 48 years and in 1971 received the British Empire Medal for his dedication.

Throughout this period the village population hovered around the 900 mark, but the process of new houses for old continued. The first council houses were built in Empson's Loke in 1925, and Edward Bush established the Bush Estate in the late 1930s. It was at this time that the quality of life in the village started to improve with the introduction of basic public services. In April 1930

77. Hauling the lifeboat *Eleanor Brown*, c1910. There are over 40 men holding the rope, showing why the boat was unpopular with the beachmen. The yawl *Band of Hope* is to be seen in the background.

a start was made on laying electricity cables and on the 20th August the first domestic electric light was switched on, replacing the traditional oil lamps and candles. In August 1934 a public telephone box was installed near the chapel and later that year water supply pipes were laid. Prior to this water had been drawn from wells, with those who owned them charging others for their use. The first policeman was stationed in the village in 1935.

A number of warehouses were built for the new boat owners with those of Powley Dick, Jack Roker, and Walter Scuddy being erected near their houses in Bulmer Lane. Robert Rudd and the Powles brothers established theirs to the west of the church, and Social set his up near to that of his brother on North Market Road.

Though not a building, something was created at this time which had great significance to a community so dependent on the sea and that was the Fisherman's Corner in the Parish Church. This was the brainchild of the Rev. Clarence Porter, who took a great interest in the seafaring activities of the village, even overcoming superstition to go to sea to find out what it was like to be a herring fisherman. The Corner was set up in 1927 as a memorial to those fishermen who had lost their lives since the First World War. Nine names are recorded, men who were lost between 1919 and 1936. The central feature in the Corner is a cross made from ship's timbers, around which has been placed a collection of nautical items, including a piece of drift net. Sadly, on 7th July 1932, Porter lost his life whilst rescuing Douglas George, one of his choirboys, who had got into difficulties while swimming off the beach.

Involvement in the herring fishery dominated every aspect of Winterton life. At the top of the deep-sea fishing hierarchy was the boat owner, in good times the wealth creator for the whole village. Some ran their businesses from Yarmouth but most found it easier and cheaper to work from home, something that was particularly beneficial to the village womenfolk.

That the boat owners were skippers who had worked their way up has already been made clear. Many owned one boat and continued to skipper for themselves, but those who possessed more than one had to find skippers. Naturally enough owners wanted the best and the best wanted the pick of the boats, good gear and, if they were extra special, a bonus on top of their share of the money made on the voyage.

The most successful were referred to as 'lucky' skippers but, while luck came into it, success was more often than not down to good management. Freddy Brown of Caister (of Winterton migrant stock) had a reputation throughout the fleet as a lucky skipper. Because his many brothers were already successful skippers when he obtained his ticket in 1927, he received three offers of boats at a time when many skippers were getting none. Advised by his brothers, he chose the newest, the *Golden Sunbeam*, owned by Jack George. Freddy started with old gear, but did well enough to move on to boats with better gear, a key requirement for success, for it was wisely said that nets caught fish not boats.

Freddy, in the *Paradox*, and Powley Dick, in the *Broadland*, once went to the 'Westards', as fishing from the West Country ports was termed. The *Broadland* was a newer boat, but had old nets. The *Paradox*, with new nets, did much better. Old nets became misshapen in the water enabling the fish to slip through the mesh or fall out when the nets were hauled. New nets were essential in bad weather, but they were not popular with the men, as they had to be tanned on board, while the boat was in harbour.

The owner would leave it to his skipper to choose a crew, men who worked on a share basis and were paid by results. The money from a voyage would be divided into 16 parts, nine of which would go to the owner and the remainder to the crew. There were normally 10 men to a boat, with the skipper getting a one and three-quarter share, the mate and driver one and a quarter shares each,

78. The Rev. William Green, left, and the Rev. Clarence Porter, right, c1920.

79. 'Powley Dick' Green, left, and Valentine Larner, right, 1914. Taken on the 'Westards'.

the hausermen one share, the stoker and the two three-quarter and half-quarter men, what that name implies, the two yonkers a three-quarter share each, and the cook half a share.

The cook was usually a lad of about 15 and it was in this role that most Winterton fishermen started out. Getting this first berth depended very much on personal connections. If the boy came from a longstanding fishing family then he would usually be offered a berth at the right time. Otherwise things would be more difficult.

Geoffrey Wacy was from a 'new family' and when he left school, several of his schoolmates easily got berths, but not him. One day he was standing near the Stone among a crowd of fishermen when he heard that George Dyble was taking out the *Girl Pamela* as a first time skipper. Running all the way to The Clink, Geoffrey knocked on Dyble's door and asked if he needed a cook. Fortunately he did and Geoffrey was signed on.

At the beginning of his maiden voyage the crew spent three days getting ready before setting off. When they did finally get underway they got no further than Gorleston, where the boat was moored and everyone, except Geoffrey, hurried into the William IV. Left to prepare the meal he put the crockery and the cutlery into a bucket and, having washed the dishes, shot the dirty water over the side, cutlery and all. He could have wept.

The same principles applied to the recruitment of the other crew members. Mates with brothers who were successful skippers were always in demand and drivers were usually relatives who, for whatever reason, were not destined to become skippers.

Winterton fishermen preferred a berth with a Winterton skipper, for the boat was likely to have good gear and they would know most of the crew. Skippers would rarely have to approach anyone for the non-specialist crew roles, for men would come to them. This would usually be in one or other of the inns and skippers rarely had to buy a drink before a voyage. These berths would often be filled by non-Winterton men, who would arrive in the village around Good Friday or later in the year, after the harvest. These were the 'greenhands' who did most of the heavy work on a fishing voyage.

With the gear stowed and the crew aboard, the steam drifter was ready to leave for the fishing grounds. Most owners designated the ports from which their skippers were to fish, leaving them to decide where to go from there, but Wee Green would send telegrams to his skippers at the various ports telling them exactly where to fish.

The voyage pattern at this time took the drifters around the whole of the British Isles. This is demonstrated by reference to trips made by the *Rose and Gladys* in 1928. She had just become the sole property of Starchy Jnr., who was also running the *Golden Gain* at the time. The narrative draws on notes made in a small diary.[58]

For the first three months of the year both boats were in Yarmouth harbour and a man named Grimmer was paid for 'watching'. During that time repairs were carried out, boilers cleaned, and new gear purchased. In March the *Rose and Gladys* went into dry dock for minor repairs and painting. On the 31st March she set off for Milford Haven and on the 29th May nine of her nets were sent back to Yarmouth for mending via the *Ocean Trust*.

Two days later she was at Dunmore in Southern Ireland. From there she moved to Buncranna, in Northern Ireland (8th June), then Castlebay, on the Island of Barra (20th June), before arriving at Lerwick in the Shetlands on the 26th June. Just prior to this, 45 more nets were sent back via the *Jack George*. Catches were generally small with the best being 53½ cran on the 8th June, which sold for £135.1s.9d. While at Lerwick a catch of 81 cran only made £30 and 20 cran had to be dumped.

On the 17th July the *Rose and Gladys* was at Fraserburgh and by the 10th August she was fishing from Peterhead. The income was steady but some days the boat made nothing at all. On the 10th

80. Regulars outside The Three Mariners, c1910. Left to right; Funky Bowgin, ——, Harry Larner, Robert Sheals, George King (innkeeper), Eli Waters, Jimmy Moll, George Haylett, Billy Larner, Joe Lown, Billy Haylett, George Smith, Edgar Hodds, Charlie Moll, Sid Haylett, and Charles Larner.

81. Steam drifter *Rose and Gladys* YH 875, entering Yarmouth harbour, c1930. She was owned by Jack 'Starchy' George Jnr..

September she arrived back in Yarmouth, returning to dry dock for repairs. Her income from the voyage was £1,028.

On the 17th September she started the home fishing with 108 nets. From then on the entries are fairly clipped, merely noting the number of cran caught, the income received and the number of 'spoilt' (damaged) nets, which was in double figures most days. Reference is also made to tanning the nets and their cartage by the carriers. She finished on the 17th December having made £2,400 for a total catch of 1,467 cran. On the 20th December Starchy Jnr. banked £500 received from his fish salesman.

With most of the Yarmouth drifters following this pattern, it is easy to see that for much of the year the majority of the younger Winterton men were away, leaving their womenfolk to manage things back home. The women did much more than bring up the children, for they had a key role to play in the fishing industry and that was net mending, or 'beating' as it was termed. The point was made earlier that nets caught fish not boats and that it was important to keep them in good repair. This meant regular work for women called 'beatsters'.

Beating was carried out in the owner's warehouse. The later ones were single storey affairs, which were considered to be better because the nets did not have to be carried up and down the stairs. Many of the earlier warehouses had two storeys, with the beating done in the upper chamber and the gear stored and maintained in the lower. When the nets were brought back from Yarmouth the ransacker would pick out the least spoilt and give them to the head beatster, who would distribute them to the others. Once mended the ransacker would check them, before fixing the norzels to the ropes, although schoolboys were often paid to do this work. The beatsters were usually relations of the owner, as various group photographs show, and this kept the money in the family.

When in 1935, at the age of 14, Marjorie Leech started as an apprentice beatster, for her uncle Roker, she received 3s.8d a week from which 2d was deducted for a stamp and, after giving her grandmother 3s.0d for her keep, she was left with 6d. After six months' experience, her wage increased to 5s.8d and after another six months to 11s.4d. It rose again to 15s.2d and she would have progressed to the full rate of 22s.6d had Roker not gone out of business. Her working day was from 8.30 am until 5.00 pm, Monday to Friday, plus Saturday mornings.

Once a year, and each time they were mended, the nets were tanned to preserve them from rotting. This process was carried out in large coppers in which the preservative cutch was heated until it became liquefied. In this the nets would be steeped before being dried on drying rails. Those owners who did not have their own copper would hire one when required. The only surviving Winterton copper stands besides Toody's old warehouse in Bulmer Lane.

Fishing out of Yarmouth and having a warehouse in Winterton would not work unless there was a means of transporting the gear. This gave employment to the Yarmouth hauliers and the Winterton carrier, so long a vital link between the village and the town. For much of the 19th Century the number of carriers varied from one to three and they ran a daily service to and from the King's Arms, just north of St Nicholas Church. When in the 1880s Henry Smith took over, he reduced the service to four days a week and when, in 1908, Henry Mute Goffin became the carrier, he restricted the trips to Monday, Wednesday, and Saturday, later dropping the Monday run.

Mute started with a carrier's cart but, in 1923, bought a model T Ford lorry, which had a canvas cover over a metal frame. To carry passengers he had Henry Brown, the carpenter, make bench seats for which Mute's wife made the cushions. He could seat 20 but when licensing came in the number had to be reduced to 14.

82. Tarring pallets, c1910. Dennis 'Cuddy' George is on the left, Harry 'Lick' George on the right.

83. Dennis 'Cuddy' George with his beatsters, c1910. Left to right; front row, Olive Grimes, Ena Tungate, Angie Rouse. Back row, Libby Hodds, Dennis George, and Christiana Haylett.

84. Henry 'Mute' Goffin, the carrier, in one of his two-wheeled carts outside the Fisherman's Return, c1905. The lad with him is a young 'Bounty' Hewitt.

His vehicles were kept in a yard alongside his house, north of the Back Path. When he moved to Miriam Terrace he built a shed to the rear of the property, which acted as a depot for goods to be despatched and collected. Women would send their grocery orders to Yarmouth via Mute, who would take them to the shop. The shopkeeper would deliver the completed orders to the King's Arms for Mute to pick up and convey back to his shed for collection. The tallyman's orders were dealt with in the same fashion.

For the 'longshoremen he would cart the fish off the beach in trunks and take them to the Yarmouth fish market. For the deep-sea fishermen he provided a number of services. Carrying the nets and gear to and from Yarmouth has already been mentioned, but for the fishermen themselves he had an arrangement with the fish salesmen to bring their money back to the village. The salesmen would give Mute a cheque and a list of men to be paid with the amounts they were entitled to. He would cash the cheque and pay the money to the fishermen when they called. For this service he charged 2d in the pound. He did the same with the money sent to the families of married fishermen whilst their breadwinner was away fishing.

Transporting the fishermen was also a job for Mute. When the Winterton steam drifters passed the village on their way back to Yarmouth their whistles would blast three long and one short toot. Standing on the dunes with his telescope to his eye, Mute would spot his customers and set off to Yarmouth to pick them up. They could also telephone him when they came into port and he would go and fetch them. Tooting the whistle when passing Winterton on the way to the fishing grounds was also a popular pastime with the fishermen and their wives assembled on Bolly Wolly Hill would wave tearfully in reply.

85. The Waite Family, c1872. Left to right; Jimmy, Alice, and Emma.

86. A matchbox label advertising the Fisherman's Return. The returning fisherman is Aaron Abel King 'Roger' Goffin.

The two innkeepers also ran transport. Jimmy Waite at the Fisherman's kept a trap and a cart. Both could be booked like taxis to take people to Hemsby station. The trap, with Jubit between the shafts, would cost 1s.6d return, whereas to hire the cart would cost 2s.0d.

After a voyage the crew would 'make up', that is clear the boat of nets and gear. Each fisherman could then return home to his family, but his first port of call in the village would usually be the aptly named Fisherman's Return. With money to spend he would, like as not, have already been drinking in Yarmouth. Throwing his money onto the bar counter he would cry 'drinks all round'. Emma, Jimmy Waite's redoubtable wife, who really ran the inn, would serve the man a pint, taking the appropriate amount of money before scooping the rest back into his leather pouch and placing it in a mug with his name on it under the bar counter. Eventually the drunken fisherman would go home to his wife and an almighty row for not bringing any money home. The following day the dejected man would return to the inn, saying to Emma. 'I can't think where all my money went'. Emma would smile and produce the pouch. The overjoyed fisherman would offer her half the money, but she would tell him to take it home to his wife. Sometimes it was the wife who turned up knowing what Emma did for the long-suffering womenfolk of the village.

Emma would often sort out brawls on the basis that it would be safer for her to do so than Jimmy. Men would take more from her than they would from a man, but Jimmy was not so sure. When he was on lifeboat duty, he would ask Bob the Devil Green to look out for Emma. One day one of the men grabbed her by the collar as if to throttle her. Bob immediately took hold of him and would have shaken him lifeless if Emma had not intervened. Throwing the man down Bob exclaimed, 'You're not fit to touch such a fine woman as Emma'.

Emma's granddaughter, Kitty George, and her husband Jack Shivvy, kept the Fisherman's from

1928 and it is still referred to by some as Shivvy's. It was Kitty's opinion that many of her clientele were selfish cruel old men who were only interested in drinking, fighting, and fornicating. These, of course, would be the Devil's Den men.

Besides beating and net braiding, the other paying work for the village women was gansey knitting, although this was often carried out as a necessity for their menfolk. A gansey (a type of woollen jumper) was an essential part of a fisherman's clothing as it kept him warm and dry while allowing him to move freely because it was knitted in the round.

Over the years patterns evolved to identify the wearer's village, family, and even how many children he had. They were in fact the fisherman's coat of arms. There was a good practical reason for these patterns for if a fisherman was washed overboard and his body came ashore further down the coast, the people finding it could identify where he was from.

Ganseys were knitted commercially and during this period Johnsons of Yarmouth used to pay for them to be made as out-work. The wool would be brought to Mrs. Brown's shop at the top of The Loke and she would organise the work. Knitters were allowed a month to complete a gansey and got 4s.0d for each one. Children would help by knitting the plain pieces. Each month a man would arrive from Johnsons to collect the completed work. Gansey knitting more or less died out before the Second World War, but the last knitter in Winterton was the well-known Casey Goffin, who had learned the skill from his mother, Mandy.

Oiling the wheels of village life was a number of services and trades. In 1929 there were two butchers, a baker, two shopkeepers, (one of whom was also the post master), a grocer, a fish curer, two cobblers, a coal merchant, a builder, a ladies' hairdresser and, perhaps surprisingly, a cycle dealer. Some of these men had disabilities and, in accordance with the brutal frankness of the time,

87. William 'Casey' Goffin, c1975. He is wearing a gansey he knitted himself.

88. A horse-brake with tourists outside the Fisherman's Return, c1905. The man holding the horse's head is 'Blind Harry' Powles.

had nicknames that highlighted the fact. These included Lame Jimmy King and John Hopknee King, but the most celebrated of them all was Blind Harry Powles.

When Harry was a youngster he received severe burns, which resulted in him becoming totally blind. Provided with glass eyes he rarely used them as he felt more comfortable without. As a consequence he always kept his eyelids closed. When old enough to earn a living he was sent to Norwich to learn basket making, but on his return he lost interest in the trade and secured a job as a yardman on the local estate. This involved feeding, grooming, and riding the horses, something he accomplished with ease, as he seemed to have an affinity with them. Skilled in this way he moved on to become the groom at the Fisherman's Return, where he would unhitch, feed, and water the horses of the four-in-hand brakes that in summer would come out from Yarmouth with tourists.

Later still he set himself up as a coal merchant, even though it involved travelling to Hemsby station to unload coal from a railway truck. Seeing him on his rounds people found it hard to believe he was blind. Not only did he know where each customer lived, but he would also unerringly go straight to their coal shed. His determination to overcome adversity and his remarkable skill made him a popular character in the village.

6. 1939 TO THE PRESENT DAY

As far as Great Britain was concerned the Second World War officially started on the 3rd September 1939. For Winterton this meant a repeat of the events of 25 years earlier, when the naval reservists were called up and the village owned drifters were requisitioned for war service.

As luck would have it, the central depot for the Royal Naval Patrol Service, in which many of the RNR men would serve, was established a few miles down the coast at the Sparrow's Nest in Lowestoft. It was the nearest British military establishment to Nazi-occupied Europe.

The Winterton men who had opted for the Patrol Service reported to the Nest. From there they were posted to the various requisitioned and purpose built trawlers, drifters, and other small craft, to carry out mine-sweeping, submarine chasing, and harbour work in home waters and around the world.

Skipper Bob the Devil Green Jnr. joined the RNR in March 1938. On the outbreak of war he returned from Milford Haven, where he had been trawling since 1931, and was given command of an Icelandic trawler, the *Kingston Chrysoberyl*, stationed at Belfast. In 1943 he was promoted to skipper-lieutenant and was placed in command of the newly built trawler *Macbeth*, employed in sub-chasing and convoy work. With the war over he continued to sweep the channels around the Isle of Wight until demobbed in early 1946.

Toody Jnr. was posted to the Winterton drifter *Triumph*, off the Nore. She was the floating anchor point for a barrage balloon and as such was a target for German parachute mines.

Not all Winterton fishermen were in the RNR, but on call-up most went into the Royal Navy or the Patrol Service. Geoffrey Wacy was one such man. Called up and sent to the Nest, he was posted to the Lowestoft drifter *Sunnyside Girl* on harbour duties at Scapa Flow, where a German U-boat had sunk the aircraft carrier *Ark Royal*. After further training back at Lowestoft he returned to Scapa

89. The steam drifter *Romany Rose* YH63, Yarmouth harbour, 1947, the year after her Prunier Trophy win. Left to right; —-, 'Tooshy' Brown, 'Buster' from Overstrand, —-, Harold Larner (mate), and Walter 'Toody' Rudd (skipper owner). On the wheelhouse is Mr. Flinders (compass adjuster), and Mr. Laurie (electrician).

Flow, to the drifter *Deliverer*, which was acting as a messenger for the battleship *King George V*.

This was followed by a compassionate posting to the Icelandic trawler *Niblick*, which was patrolling between Yarmouth and Blakeney. She was later sent to Grimsby to be camouflaged for towing decoy barges from Southampton to Leith. She also towed dummy landing craft, made of oil drums and canvas, to Boulogne and sent them onto the beaches where the Germans 'knocked hell out of them'.

The *Niblick* was next employed sweeping ahead of the Normandy invasion fleet. Returning to British waters she was sent to sweep from Plymouth to Dartmouth, then Plymouth to Falmouth before Geoffrey was posted to another Icelandic trawler, the *Rosslade*, fitted to deal with magnetic mines. Patrolling between Grimsby and Blakeney, she located 12 such mines and was still sweeping when the Germans surrendered. Shortly afterwards, while working off Portland Bill in thick fog, an American liberty ship, the *Sydney Sherman*, sank another sweeper and hit and damaged the *Rosslade*. She limped off to Liverpool where, in December 1945, Geoffrey was demobbed.

Not all were as fortunate as these men who survived the lottery of war for, with the conflict over, 26 more names were added to the village war memorial, including those of two women, Katy Brown and Edna Hodds, killed when the Luftwaffe bombed the village.

Fearing invasion, the order was given for potential landing beaches to be defended. Once mined, Winterton beach was cordoned off with barbed wire and scaffolding and people could be, and were, fined, for unauthorised entry. Concrete tank traps and pillboxes were constructed and the lighthouse tower became a lookout for a gun emplacement on the cliff. On the Bush estate a 350 feet high radar mast was erected, thought to have been used to direct mosquito pilots, acting as pathfinders on bombing raids. On the Common, to the north of the village, a dummy town and aerodrome was set up with fake lights, which Nimble Empson was employed to look after. It was intended to mislead German night raiders into thinking they were looking at Yarmouth. The ruse worked, but the gun emplacement and radar mast were obvious daytime targets, which seems to have been the reason why on the 6th May 1943 the village was attacked.

At 6.15 a.m. two German bombers flew in at low level, from the north, and each dropped a bomb. The first went clean through a bedroom of Henry Smith's house in Providence Row, bounced in The Lane, just ahead of Eddie George, who was riding along on his bike, before striking a telegraph pole, exploding, and bringing down two cottages near the Fisherman's Return. Fortunately no one was killed.

The second bomb bounced between Miriam Terrace and Snowdrop Cottages before hitting a row of houses in The Alley. A contemporary Eastern Daily Press report picks up the story; 'There were many examples of courage when an East Anglian coast village was bombed yesterday, and outstanding among them was the fortitude of a ten-year-old girl, Stella Hodds, buried among the ruins of her burning home.

Mr. Empson, a part-time member of the Royal Observer Corps, who extricated Stella, described her as the pluckiest child he had ever encountered. "I shouted into the ruins of the thatched cottage," he told a reporter, "and heard the girl say, I am here, but I can't move and can't see a thing. Can you see my hand?"

"There were some tiny fingers sticking out of a pile of bricks and timber. When I succeeded in pulling the rubble away the girl leapt into my arms".

The ruins were burning and villagers successfully formed a chain of buckets to keep the flames from the girl and her rescuer.

Stella was in her bedroom when the house collapsed. She was uninjured, but the body of her crippled mother, Mrs. Edna Hodds, was later recovered. She was downstairs when the cottage was struck.

In another house Mrs. K. Brown, a widow, was killed, and her sister, Mrs. Goffin, severely

90. Motor fishing boat *Brenjean* YH385, 1949. Owned by 'Bob the Devil' Green Jnr. and Bob 'Shammy' Haylett.

injured. Mrs. Goffin's husband, a merchant seaman, surprised helpers by crawling from the remains of the house unhurt.

Several homes were virtually demolished and a number of others damaged. A Methodist chapel also suffered.

Ten casualties were treated in the windowless rooms of the first aid post... Hot meals were sent to the village by mobile canteens and a squad of repairers arrived from a nearby town'.[59]

Ironically it was Alfred Pamp Hodds, the husband of one of the dead women, who being on Observer Corps duty, spotted the two planes and immediately alerted Ludham aerodrome. Fighters were scrambled and the German raiders were caught as they were heading out to sea. One of them was shot down. Later the RAF pilot responsible visited Pamp to congratulate him on his promptness. It must have been a bittersweet moment.

With the war over, the fishermen came home and the surviving requisitioned drifters were returned to their owners. But, during the black days before the war, many of the men had forsaken the unpredictable life of a fisherman for the other extreme, regular employment with a public authority or statutory undertaker. This trend continued after the war with men taking jobs with the Catchment Board, fire service, waterworks and Trinity House. A writer in 1950 commented that there were now not more than 30 men engaged in the fishing.

As for the Winterton owned drifters only four resumed fishing, the *Triumph*, the *Ocean Swell*, the *Rose Hilda*, and the *Romany Rose*. The *Brenjean* joined them in 1948; the last newly owned Winterton deep-sea fishing boat.

Absolom Abbs Goffin skippered the *Triumph* until September 1951, when she was broken up. Wee Green's *Ocean Swell* was the first boat to land herring at Yarmouth after the war, with a haul of 15 cran, on the 7th October 1945. He had resumed his fishing business in Yarmouth, but on his death in early 1949 his son Eddie took over and ran the boats from Winterton until the home fishing of 1953. By then he had come to the conclusion that the fishing was over so he called it a day. The *Ocean Swell* was sold to Belgium for breaking up and the *Rose Hilda* went to work at Lowestoft under the name *Dawn Waters* (LT90).

The Brenjean, owned by Bob the Devil Jnr. and Bob Shammy Haylett, was built towards the end of the war as a motor fishing boat for the Patrol Service. Such boats were sold after the war to ex-servicemen who were given a government loan to start up and would be entitled to a grant of £5,000, should they survive in business for five years. The boat was named after their daughters, Brenda and Jean.

There was not time to net her for the home fishing of 1948 so they went trawling at Milford Haven until the home fishing of 1949, when Arthur Moore of Rollesby netted the boat. They never netted her themselves and therefore did not need a warehouse. In 1950 the same pattern was followed, with the boat being netted by a Lowestoft firm, but the voyage was not a success so the firm put in its own skipper and sent the *Brenjean* to Scotland for deep-sea lining. In 1956 she was sold by the Herring Industry Board to recover debts.

Toody Jnr. was demobbed in time to take the *Romany Rose* to sea for the home fishing of 1945. After five years of war there was an abundance of fish and he had a good voyage, grossing between £8,000 and £9,000.

The next year, 1946, the *Romany Rose* became the first Yarmouth boat to win the coveted Prunier Trophy and Toody the first Winterton man to do so. The Prunier Trophy was the idea of restaurateur Madame Prunier, who wanted to promote the herring as a food. It was awarded to the boat landing the biggest catch of fresh herring in one shot at either Yarmouth of Lowestoft, during a set period. First awarded in 1936, it lapsed during the war years and Toody's was the first post-war award.

On the 4th November 1946 the *Romany Rose* made the winning catch of 245¾ cran, 30 miles N.E. of the Cockle Gat. Her crew was engaged for 23 hours from the start of hauling to that of landing, and at auction the shot made a useful £950.

91. Crew of the steam drifter *Romany Rose* YH63, North Shields, c1948. Left to right; back row, —-, Bob Green, Walter 'Toody' Rudd (skipper/owner), Johnny Goffin (mate), —-, Eddie Hodds, Front row, —-, Shill Haylett, —-, and —-.

92. Presentation of the Prunier Trophy and weathervane to the crew of the *Ocean Starlight* YH61, December 1962. Left to right; E. George, J. Grimson, P. Nickerson, the Mayoress, W. J. Rembrance, C. Dane, Stanley 'Bounty' Hewitt, (skipper), B. Rogers, John Birchenall, Mayor of Great Yarmouth, Victor Powles, Eddie Hodds, and R. Tough.

Toody continued fishing until 1955, but with motor vessels taking over and the fish stocks declining, he too decided enough was enough. The *Romany Rose* was broken up the following year, bringing to a close Winterton's long history of deep-sea fishing boat ownership.

The herring fishery struggled on, with landings decreasing season by season, the problem being put down to unrestricted trawling by foreign vessels and the taking of immature fish. Some Winterton men, however, continued to crew the Yarmouth boats and it is one of these, Bounty Hewitt, who signed off the Winterton fishing tradition in style.

Bounty had been a successful skipper and boat owner during the 1930s, but his boat, the *Young Ernie*, was sunk off the Tyne during the war. On demobilisation he skippered the *Animation* for George Newson until 1955, when Newson, who was Winterton based for a while, finished with the fishing. Bounty had a short spell ashore before skippering the *Ocean Starlight* for Bloomfields. It was in her, in 1962, that he became the second Winterton skipper to win the Prunier Trophy.

Late on the evening of the 9th November, after a ten-hour haul, Bounty arrived in Yarmouth harbour with a shot of 294⅓ cran, caught 40 miles E. by N. of Smith's Knoll. The catch fetched £1,100. At the end of that season, at the age of 66, Bounty retired. Four years later the last Prunier Trophy was awarded and the once great Yarmouth herring fishery was no more.

That the seafaring days of Winterton were virtually over was recognised as early as 1949, in an Eastern Dairy Press article entitled. 'Winterton's Fishermen are leaving the Sea'.[60] This was reinforced the following year by a Yarmouth Mercury feature, 'Portrait of a Village: Winterton Lives on Its Own'.[61]

Both pieces highlighted the fact that there were now few active fishermen. It was also noted that; 'Fewer still go 'longshoring although 86-year-old Bob Burton helps to take a boat to sea from Yarmouth'.[62] In addition, mention was made of the fact that; 'there was a time when Winterton lifeboats – it had two, and eight coastguards as well – were launched almost directly into the sea. Now the sheds, long empty of their craft, are 200 to 300 yards from breakers'.[63]

The old rivalry between the two groups of beachmen also resurfaced, but in the guise of 'rival gangs of singing fishermen' who had their headquarters in the two inns. At the time of these articles the leader of the Winterton singers was 72-year-old Sam Funky Larner. Sam was little known outside the village, but in 1956 he was 'discovered' in the Fisherman's Return by Philip Donnellan, a BBC producer. Donnellan was quick to recognise the importance of Sam as a folk-singer and also the antiquity of his songs, many of which featured fishing and the sea. These he recorded in Sam's home and the BBC went as far as to say that Sam was considered to be one of the greatest folk singers to come to light for many years.

As something of a celebrity Sam appeared on television and radio and the recordings were issued as long playing records, but arguably his most important piece of work was the contribution he made to the radio ballad, 'Singing the Fishing'. This was produced by Ewan Maccoll and Charles Parker and is a must for anyone interested in Winterton and the herring fishery. Sam died in 1965, his only regret being that he had not been discovered sooner.

Some people in the late 1940s still felt that the future of the village lay with the beach and the sea, but for holidaymakers not fishing. This was a view shared by Kenneth Temple who in 1948 bought Hill House, by then in a derelict state as it had been used by the army during the war. With this as the focal point he created the Hotel Hermanus complex, with its distinctive rondavals, based on the design of the Zulu kraal, the inspiration for which came to him on a visit to Hermanus Bay in South Africa. When in 1972 he sold his holding it comprised the hotel, 42 furnished houses, bungalows and flats, the lighthouse, and 50 acres of sand hills, together with the beach above the high-water mark. The dwellings included 12 thatched and colour washed houses opposite the Fisherman's Return, which had received an architectural design award. The Hermanus complex is still a thriving concern today.

In 1951 the first post war census revealed a parish population of just over 900 people, much the same as it has been for the previous 40 years. Ten years later the figure had dropped to 824, perhaps reflecting the impact the demise of the fishing industry had had on village employment and community life. The housing stock had, as a result, remained static, once the 22 houses demolished in the war had been more than replaced by pre-fabs and Airey houses.

Since then the village has proved attractive to retired people and commuters to Yarmouth and elsewhere. In the past few decades a number of new housing developments have encouraged the population to grow to close on 1,500 people.

Today Winterton retains the excellent coastal setting it has always possessed, with one of the finest beaches in Norfolk. The sea-bank still protects the village, although recent erosion has been a cause for concern, and from it the volunteer organisation, Coastwatch, maintains the age-old tradition of lifesaving.

The village is a comfortable, relatively unspoilt, place, and to those who know where to look, its maritime heritage is everywhere, standing as a monument to that hardy race of seafaring men and women who for centuries were proud to call Winterton their home.

Notes and References

1 Hoskins, W. G., Fieldwork in Local History, 1967 pp79-85 and Cornford, Barbara, Medieval Flegg, 2002, pp 21-22.

2 Sawyer, P.H., Anglo-Saxon Charters, 1968, pp 315-316.

3 Domesday Book, Norfolk, Phillimore, 1984.

4 Hood, C.M., The Chorography of Norfolk, 1938, p170.

5 Cornford, p187.

6 Close Rolls, Edward III, Aug 20th 1360, Mem. 15d.

7 State Papers, Westminster 8th Nov 1565.

8 Norwich Consistory Court Inventories, 1591, DN/INV8/270.

9 Muster of Seamen, 21st December 1664, Raynham Hall.

10 Norwich Archdeaconry Wills, 1711-12, 268.

11 The Paston Letters, Ed. James Gairdner, 1897, Vol III letter 807.

12 Defoe, Daniel, A Tour Through the Whole Island of Great Britain, Penguin edition, 1971, p 92.

13 Defoe, pp 93-94.

14 NRO, BR90/12.

15 Defoe, p 94.

16 Yarmouth Independent 14th Aug 1880.

17 NRO, BR 90/12/10.

18 Cornford, B., Hemsby in the Later Middle Ages. Norf. Research Com. Bulletin No32, Sept 1984.

19 White's Directory of Norfolk, 1836 p 317.

20 Long, Neville, Lights of East Anglia, 1983, pp 49-50.

21 Eastern Daily Press 5th January 1935.

22 National Archives. High Court of Delegates, DEL 7/2, Fols 234-244.

23 National Archives, Cust. 97/29-30.

24 Papers of the Great Yarmouth Admiralty Court, NRO, C16/16/5.

25 Preston, The Picture of Yarmouth, 1819, p 234.

26 A study of title deeds would reveal much about the village and, coupled with knowledge of boat owners, could well reveal earlier fishing related buildings.

27 R[obert] P[orter], The Strangers Guide Book for the Polite Village of Martham, 1830. Manuscript book, NRO, MC 90/1, p 122.

28 P[orter], p 121.

29 The Spreading Flame, Cyril Jolly, n.d, p 87.

30 Edward Norton Larner, Memories of Fifty years.

31 Chapters on the East Anglian Coast, John Greaves Nall, 1866, Vol 1 p 421.

32 National Archives. High Court of Admiralty, HCA 7/21.

33 ibid.

34 Eastern Daily Press 12th March 1990.

35 Northumberland Report on lifeboats, 1851.

36 Norwich Mercury 9th August 1851.

37 Higgins, David, Captain George King and the Winterton to Goole Migration, Norfolk Ancestor, June 1994.

38 Clarke, William M., The Secret Life of Wilkie Collins, 1988.

39 White's Directory of Norfolk, 1845, p 306.

40 Nall, p 421.

41 NRO, D41/65. May Gale Relief Fund.

42 Yarmouth Independent 14th August 1880.

43 ibid.

44 Yarmouth Independent 9th Jan 1875.

45 Yarmouth Independent 16th Jan 1875.

46 Norwich Mercury 31st Oct 1868.

47 Transcript kindly provided by John Green MBE.

48 I am grateful to Brian Rudd for this explanation.

49 Yarmouth Independent 30th Jan 1875.

50 Yarmouth Independent 19th Jan 1889.

51 Yarmouth Independent 24th Oct 1891.

52 Yarmouth Independent 31st Oct 1891.

53 Trans. of the Norf. and Norwich Naturalists Soc., 1899, p 482.

54 Fishermen in War Time, Walter Wood, n.d, p 47.

55 Service Record, National Archives   BT 377/14.

56 Trans. of the Norf. and Norwich Naturalists Soc., 1929, p 669.

57 Long, p 50.

58 The diary is in my possession but will shortly be deposited in the Norfolk Record Office.

59 Eastern Daily Press 8th May 1943.

60 Eastern Daily Press 18th June 1949.

61 Yarmouth Mercury 26th May 1950.

62 Eastern Daily Press 18th June 1949.

63 ibid.

Index of Vessels

Refuge (lifeboat)	37	Stately (man-of-war)	18	Vulcan	29
Rescuer (lifeboat)	43	Sunnyside Girl (sd)	83	W Elliott YH423 (sd)	58,65,**65**
Reserve No 1 (lifeboat)	47	Supporter YH74 (sd)	68,70	Wikenger (brig)	33
Resurge YH21 (sd)	69	Sweet Bud YH174 (sd)	71	William	17,43
Robert and John YH858 (dandy)	52,54,56,58	Sweet Pea YH924 (sd)	58	William and Ann (beach boat)	41
Romany Rose YH63 (sd)		Syble (SS)	45	William Tell (lugger)	37
	68,70,**83**,85,86,**86**,87	Sydney Sherman (liberty ship)	84	Wonder (brig)	30
Rose and Gladys YH875 (sd)	67,71,76,**77**	Tally Ho (beach boat)	41	WPG YH174 (sd)	66,71
Rose Hilda YH73 (sd)	68,85	Teal (SS)	46	Yare (steam-tug)	45
Rosslade (trawler)	84	Theodor (barque)	46	Young Archie YH291 (sd)	58
Rover (beach boat)	41	Thirty-Two YH709 (sd)	67	Young Ernie YH55 (sd)	69,87
Ruby (barque)	43	Thistle (brig)	27	Young Fox (ketch)	46
Scud (brigantine)	44	Tom Perry (steam-tug)	45	Young Greyhound (yawl)	26,34,44
Shah (beach boat)	41	Triumph YH568 (sd)	70,71,83,85	Young Recruit (beach boat)	41
Silver Spray YH175 (sd)	58,**63**	Troas (beach boat)	41		
Speedwell (lugger)	13	True Briton (lugger)	13	HMD = His Majestys Drifter	
Sphinx YH475 (sd)	69	Twenty-Eight YH681 (sd)	66,67	mfb = motor fishing boat	
St. Beit (ship)	26	Two Brothers YH426 (lugger)	50,51,53	sd = steam drifter	
Star (steam-tug)	45	Viking YH309 (sd)	68		
Star (yawl)	33	Vriende Broder	14